Character Forged
From Conflict

THE PASTOR'S SOUL SERIES

DAVID L. GOETZ • GENERAL EDITOR

The Power of Loving Your Church
David Hansen

Pastoral Grit
Craig Brian Larson

Preaching With Spiritual Passion
Ed Rowell

Listening to the Voice of God
Roger Barrier

Leading With Integrity
Fred Smith, Sr.

Character Forged From Conflict
Gary D. Preston

LIBRARY OF LEADERSHIP DEVELOPMENT

MARSHALL SHELLEY • GENERAL EDITOR

Leading Your Church Through Conflict and Reconciliation
Renewing Your Church Through Vision and Planning
Building Your Church Through Counsel and Care
Growing Your Church Through Training and Motivation

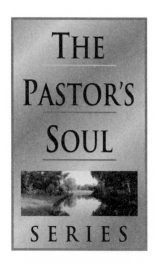

THE
PASTOR'S
SOUL

SERIES

Character Forged
From Conflict

GARY D ᐧ PRESTON

David L. Goetz ᐧ General Editor

BETHANY HOUSE PUBLISHERS
MINNEAPOLIS, MINNESOTA 55438

Published by Bethany House Publishers
A Ministry of Bethany Fellowship International
11400 Hampshire Avenue South
Minneapolis, Minnesota 55438
www.bethanyhouse.com

Printed in the United States of America by
Bethany Press International, Minneapolis, Minnesota 55438

ISBN 1–55661–973–1

Affectionately dedicated to my loving wife, Suzanne,
who twenty years ago chose to spend
the rest of her life with me,
and who brings God's grace to me
in ways I never thought possible.

GARY PRESTON is pastor of Bethany Baptist Church in Boulder, Colorado. He has written for LEADERSHIP and *Discipleship Journal*. Gary and his wife, Suzanne, enjoy a Colorado outdoor lifestyle along with their two teenage sons, Nate and Tim.

Contents

Acknowledgments....9

Introduction....11

1 / Forced Out....17

2 / Playing Hurt....35

3 / Keeping Enemies Close....49

4 / Resisting the Urge to Strike Back....61

5 / Preaching Through Controversy....73

6 / What Your Family Needs....91

7 / Staying Balanced....103

8 / Angels in the Roil....115

9 / When to Back Off....129

10 / Out of the Pain....145

ACKNOWLEDGMENTS

MY WIFE ONCE COMMENTED that although she chose me as her husband, she certainly did not choose our vocation as pastor and pastor's wife. She said, "That somehow got thrown into the package at no extra charge."

Over the years we have learned that there is often a heavy price to pay in pastoral ministry. Much of *Character Forged From Conflict* narrates our story. No doubt there are significant rewards and great joys in ministry. However, if the growing number of pastors who leave church ministry is any indication, it seems that the price may be higher than the joy is deep.

Writing this book has been my attempt to help fellow pastors regain passion for their calling, which may have cooled because of the battles and bruises of pastoral ministry. The words on these pages have been forged in the foundry of my life. Like most of my colleagues, at times I've wanted to trade the pastorate for anything else.

God has not given me permission to do that, however. At crucial times he has used some wonderful friends and fellow shepherds to renew my call and restore my vision for ministry. My wife and I are deeply grateful to Bob and Sandy Sewell, for their love and understanding of what life is like on this side of the pulpit. The Sewells are co-founders of Sonscape Ministries, a ministry of renewal in southwestern Colorado for those who minister. Were it not for the Sewells, at least from a human standpoint, I would probably be working at the U.S. Post Office instead of in the pastorate.

I also wish to acknowledge Dave Goetz at LEADERSHIP and Christianity Today, Inc., for his friendship and wise counsel over the years. Dave convinced me there was a book in some of our shared experiences in church work. His encouragement and technical guidance in writing have helped bring those experiences into written form.

Above all, I am thankful to God for the right partner he brought to me twenty years ago. It is to my loving wife, Suzanne, that I dedicate this book. Twenty years ago she chose to spend the rest of her life with me and got the role of pastor's wife thrown in! Without her love, counsel, and friendship, I would never have made it this far.

INTRODUCTION

SOME MIGHT CONTEND THAT WRITING a book on conflict in ministry is like having a divorcée invite her ex-husband over for dinner. There probably wouldn't be much peace or healing taking place during the evening. The potential would be great for old battles to be refought, hurtful memories to be uncovered, and excruciating pain of the soul to be intensified.

Character Forged From Conflict is not about winning battles or rehashing the wrongs I've suffered at the hands of parishioners. Not much good would be served in such an exercise. In fact, if that were my purpose, it would be pretty good evidence that church conflict had gained the upper hand in my soul.

Every pastor experiences conflict in ministry, some of it severe. I believe we need help in how to deal with conflict so that God can bring into our lives something good out of something bad. The Lord's brother James held out that hope for us when he wrote, "Consider it pure joy, my brothers, whenever you face trials of many kinds, because you know that the testing of your faith develops perseverance . . . so that you may be mature and complete, not lacking anything" (James 1:2–4).

A number of years ago, I heard a statement by a seasoned pastor: "In the church of Jesus Christ today, too often conflict is the norm, while peace among the brethren is the exception." At first I attributed that to ministerial hyperbole. But later I reconsidered my conclusion. Not that conflict in the church is omnipresent or the only condition of the congregations we serve, but it is inevitable and probably more common than we like to admit.

That confuses me, especially when I go back to the Gospels. In the Upper Room Discourse, Jesus told the disciples about the "peace I leave with you." He told them that their arena of conflict would be with the world. The apostle Paul wrote that peace is the one distinguishing mark of God's kingdom (Rom. 14:17). According to Galatians 5:22, peace also results from the Holy Spirit's work in our lives. The great inheritance of those who possess Christ's righteousness is peace (Rom. 5:1).

Why, then, is there so much conflict in the church?

When our two boys were younger, they went through a fighting stage. Two years apart, they seemed to think God had given them a lifelong partner for combat. One day I pulled them apart and asked, "Why are you fighting so much today?"

The older one replied, "Fighting means we love each other."

"How's that?" I asked.

"Because fighting is fun," he said with a smile.

I sometimes think the people in our churches believe that, too. Not that they head in that direction intentionally or consciously. But there are sincere saints who regularly do more harm than good, even though they are convinced they're just standing up for the truth or doing what God asks them to do. They seldom seem to back away from a good conflict. Rather than becoming salt that seasons church ministry, these pillars of piety can be bitter brine that dries our souls and drives us to the brink of abandoning our call.

That's why I am writing this book. I believe that we pastors need to be better at navigating our way through conflict in the church so we can preserve the light of God in our souls and the call of God on our lives. My prayer for this book is that in some small way, when in the dry-and-thirsty land of conflict, we can find a cleft in the rock where God can minister to us through the depths of his love and cover us there with his hand. Only when that happens can we continue to experience his grace in our souls and minister his grace amid the conflicts in the church.

1

FORCED OUT

WHEN I KNOCKED ON THE COUPLE'S massive oak door, a woman answered. Her husband was on the phone.

Her bloodshot eyes signaled immediately that this might not be the routine one-hour pastoral visit I had planned. Rick and Becky were new to the church, and I wanted to get acquainted.

"We almost canceled your visit tonight," she blurted. "Rick and I both lost our jobs this morning. Our boss came by at 9 A.M. and told us that due to corporate reshuffling 'for the good of all concerned,' our jobs were phased out as of today."

The shock, she said, was superseded only by the company's lack of compassion—they had invested fifteen years in the company. Of no one in particular, Becky asked desperately, "And how can they possibly believe this reorganization was the best for everyone involved? Who do they think they are?"

Too bad, I thought, *that corporations can't handle terminations in a more Christlike manner.*

I stayed several hours, but before leaving, I cautioned them not to make any rash decisions and then knelt beside them, concluding with a prayer that would haunt me just a few weeks later.

"Lord," I prayed, "help Rick and Becky to remain open to you during this difficult time. Give them patience to wait on you. Perhaps this is a time when you will lead them in a radically new direction."

After the prayer I sensed our time together had given them hope. On my way out, we hugged, and they said, "God knew that we needed to keep this appointment with you tonight. Thank you for your encouragement."

It was approaching midnight. As I drove home along the twisted, moonlit road, I quietly thanked the Lord for the providential visit. God would be faithful during this time of upheaval, I firmly believed, and it could be a time of significant growth for them.

I must admit, though, my mind also entertained another thought on the drive home.

Isn't it fortunate, I thought, *that the chances of that ever happening to me are remote. Sure, a host of hazards accompany the pastor's calling, but surprise terminations aren't one of them.* I felt comforted—at least I was free from *that* worry.

Six weeks later, at 10:15 one evening, our telephone rang. I picked up the phone, recognizing the voice of the board chairman.

I had expected a call. The board was meeting that evening and had promised me a late update. Earlier in the meeting, I had made a proposal to the board about how we could respond to some of the volatile issues facing the church. I informed them that I thought it best for me to resign from the church in six months so a new pastor could bring a fresh start. Affirming my commitment to the battle-weary ministry, I hoped to use the transition to bring much-needed healing to the congregation.

"The board chose me to call you tonight," the chairman began, "because I'm a good friend of yours and my wife is on the staff."

Hardly taking a breath, he continued, "The board asked me to inform you that it voted to terminate you as our pastor. We have decided to effect your intended resignation immediately."

"You mean the board is firing me?" I stammered.

"Absolutely not," he corrected. "We are only making your resignation effective tonight rather than in six months."

"What about the votes of the two absent board members?" I countered. He wasn't dissuaded; my termination was definite and immediate. In fact, he wasn't going to prolong this painful conversation either. He concluded with "the board believes this is the right decision, and it will work out best for everyone involved."

It occurred to me that I had heard similar words just weeks before.

When I hung up the phone, my wife, Suzanne, sat beside me on the bed. Even hearing only one side of the conversation, she had no difficulty figuring out what had happened. With our arms around each other, we sat in stunned silence.

"I guess we're finished here," I finally said.

With despair in her voice and tears in her eyes, she replied, "How can they do this? What are we going to do?"

LA-Z-BOY™ *depression*

I had discovered firsthand that unemployment hits pastors. This wasn't corporate restructuring, however. I was essentially fired.

For the first week I felt overcome by low-grade depression and helplessness. With little or no provocation, I would shout at our children or snap at my wife. Some days I sat paralyzed in my living room chair, barely able to answer the phone. Friends' assurances seemed hollow.

It's easy for you to tell me about God's faithfulness, I thought. *You still have your job.*

Several days passed before I could do anything other than stare into the pine forest outside our living room window. When my wife finally coaxed me out of our LA-Z-BOY™ recliner with the invitation "Would you go with me for a hike in the woods?" my recovery began. I didn't feel like leaving the security of my chair, but her patience with my anger and irritability made me feel indebted to her. Reluctantly, I gave in. Walking the trails that afternoon, I began to feel hopeful for the first time since the phone call.

Looking back, I'm certain navigating the choppy

waters of unemployment might have been easier if I had possessed a primer on pastoral unemployment. But I'd never read anything on the subject. I needed help with the myriad daily questions I was asking: *How do I explain to family, friends, and fellow pastors what happened? How do we survive financially before I find employment?*

And, of course, the ultimate question: *What is God trying to teach me through this awful experience?*

To the first question, what do we tell family and friends, we decided to be up-front, telling people we were no longer at the church, rather than to let the grapevine run its course. So we called family and close friends, relaying the facts of our termination. That was not easy. The biggest challenge was sticking only to the facts. Brief conversations, we quickly discovered, helped us do that. The longer we talked, the more likely we were to criticize people on the board or spew our volatile emotions.

When neighbors noticed I was around home every day, I informed them with a pat answer: "The church and I thought it best for both of us if I took an early retirement." They got the point and seldom asked for details.

The church promised us a severance package that would help us financially through the early weeks. Unfortunately, because of deteriorating finances and declining attendance, the church was unable to fulfill its promise. I discovered this when what turned out to be our last severance check arrived for only half the usual amount. There was no accompanying note or preparatory phone call, only half a paycheck. Once again, I felt angry and disappointed.

To fill the financial gap, I resurrected my skills as a carpenter and became a fix-it repairman. My wife was also able to add an extra day at the office where she worked part-time. The remaining shortfall God provided through special gifts from friends in the church and the community. We also found help through a ministry in southwestern Colorado called Sonscape, designed for wounded ministers and their spouses. One week there began to restore our walk with God, renewing our desire to serve again.

As I walked through the valley of unemployment, I began to learn several important lessons.

Mr. Mom

When I lost my job in ministry, I not only had to deal with loss of self-confidence and steady income but also with the losses experienced by my children, who were in elementary school at the time. They could not understand why they could not attend their church anymore and why Dad no longer preached on Sundays.

For the first six weeks after being fired, Suzanne and I couldn't bring ourselves to attend another church. At first, our two young boys were thrilled with the thought of missing church.

"Do we get to stay home from church again tomorrow, Dad?" became a routine Saturday evening question. Somehow, by not going to church, they felt naughty, like they were getting away with something.

We tried to explain. "For us, going to church is a little different than for the rest who attend our church," I told them. "Not only did we attend that church, but that is also where I was employed. So since I'm not working there anymore, it isn't okay for us to attend there."

They didn't fully understand the connection. Later they asked, "Why can't we sing in the children's choir spring concert?" and "Why isn't our family going to family camp this summer?"

Even though our boys couldn't fully grasp the significance of my termination, keeping them informed, we believed, was important. Our open communication seemed to calm the ripple effect my job loss had at home.

We also discovered a book that presents basic questions that adults who have lost a job might not think to ask their children. *When a Parent Loses a Job*, published by the National Childhood Grief Institute in Edina, Minnesota, helped our children cope with the range of emotions associated with a parent's job loss. Too often a job loss can trigger family problems and even divorce. But it need not be that way. It can be a time for a family to pull together and for the children to help the parents accept some of the grief by sharing it. The imagination of children can run wild. Children may believe worse things are going on and assume the problems are their fault.

By watching their parents, children can learn significant lessons about how to maintain a sense of hope and faith. Before going to bed, for example, our boys regularly prayed for me, asking God to help me with this difficult situation. One night our youngest petitioned, "God, help Daddy find another church to be its pastor and help him not to run over [with the car] the people on the board." The boys had a sense of my needs as well as a sense of humor.

Teens particularly can be included in many of the family discussions relating to a job loss. Of course, discretion should be used in sharing too many details when the children are present. With our preadolescent children, for example, my wife and I never used the names of board members. Though the boys were curious, we didn't think it was necessary for them to know which of their friends' parents on the board had decided to terminate me.

The boys had a hard time adjusting to our financial situation. "Dad, are we going to be poor now?" became a frequent question. I assured them that God would provide for our needs. We made a point of sharing with them the various ways God provided financially for us. When a sizable check came in the mail from a neighborhood Christian, we showed our boys the letter and the check right away.

Being on a tight budget also helped our family discern more carefully between needs and wants. We all recognized that our summer vacation plans would need to be pared down. We asked our boys, "Even though we aren't going on a big vacation this summer, do you think you still have everything you need?"

"Well, yes," they responded. "But we can hardly wait for you to get a job so we can finally get a new toy." Rather than pull them out of the Christian camp they loved, we swallowed our pride and requested financial assistance.

My unemployment was a wonderful opportunity to spend larger blocks of time with my children. I learned the art of carpooling. Walking my sons to the school bus became a morning ritual. And I joined a dozen moms from our youngest's school class to take the kids on an excursion called "A Day in Denver." Our son was the proudest kid in his class that day, the only one whose dad came along.

My wife also saw more of me. Things we had only talked about previously we now did: riding bikes, playing tennis, hiking, having lunch together. These activities enabled us to grow closer during this painful time. Without Suzanne's support, my unemployment would have been a minus rather than a plus to our family relationships. Although our money was tight, we did have extra time, and we chose to spend it freely with each other. Fortunately we owned our home and didn't feel the immediate pressure to move. Pastors who live in a parsonage may have much more complex situations to address, such as finding immediate housing and uprooting their family to a new area. We didn't have to yank our sons from their school and friends.

Not so personal

Being fired made me feel like a complete failure. I tended to accept all the blame or lay it all at the feet of the board. Neither approach was helpful. I had to acknowledge that it takes two parties to quarrel and have a parting of the ways.

I began listing mentally some of the lessons from this ordeal, trying to analyze what I could have done differently or better. That process was helpful. I recognized the debacle was partially my fault, and that was all God asked me to accept.

I also recognized that others were partly to blame as well. My journal entries during those first days following my termination were filled with angry accusations: "How could that board have been so blind and self-righteous?" But as the ink flowed from the pen to my paper, along with it went some of the anger in my soul. I recognized I should have communicated more openly with the board about the deep church problems. I also should have viewed the board, the staff, and myself as teammates rather than opponents.

No one has ever seen those written words, but as I reread them now, I recognize how my journal became my therapist. Journaling allowed me to express unrighteous thoughts and feelings. In so doing, issues such as personal responsibility, forgiveness, acceptance, and trust floated to the surface.

The loss of my job demonstrated painfully to me that I'm not in control of my life—but I needed to control what I could. Because of the demands of ministry, I had been neglecting activities that I enjoyed.

A time of unemployment can be an opportunity to eat and exercise properly. Sharpening dormant skills, cultivating a hobby, and having fun aren't sins during this kind of interim. Before our severance pay ran out, I tackled several woodworking projects that had been on hold. I built a new porch swing and picnic table. Our garage has never been more organized, and my wife's fix-it list was finally fixed.

Not only did I spend more time with my family, I spent more time with God. After that terrible phone call, one of the first friends I had lunch with challenged me to draw closer to the Lord than I had ever been. "Just because you feel ostracized from the church at this time, doesn't mean the Lord of the church isn't still longing for your friendship," he said.

That was good advice. I used the first hour of the day after our boys went to school to spend time with the Lord, and it proved to be a real gift. Rather than the quick ten- or fifteen-minute devotional time I always had at my office, I could now ask God questions and listen for answers; I read chapters instead of verses; I rediscovered the joy of using a hymnal to commune with God.

Focus on the family

My wife pointed out that when I, as a pastor, lost my job, we lost more than just a paycheck. We also lost our church family, the very community that others who are unemployed can still draw upon to find comfort, understanding, and encouragement.

Church attendance, then, was something we needed to confront. For the first six weeks after my termination, we had no desire to set foot in a church. We accepted our feelings and gave ourselves permission to treat Sunday just like our nonchurched neighbors. The only difference was that we had a time of family worship, either on Saturday evening or Sunday morning after breakfast. Then we used Sunday as a restful family day.

When we finally felt comfortable in attending a public worship service, we sought out one of the largest churches in the area, where we could be anonymous. That was a good idea. Both Suzanne and I cried our way through those initial worship services. I'm sure the people sitting around us wondered what our problem was, but at least they allowed us privacy.

Eventually we were ready to add a few personal relationships to our public worship experiences. That's when we began attending a large church where we knew a few people. We stayed there, thankful to have found a church that allowed us the freedom to heal without any pressure to be involved.

To supplement our casual church attendance,

though, we needed the support of Christian friends. My wife and I were invited to participate in two small groups. Although we declined to do so on a weekly basis, meeting with them occasionally was encouraging. We knew they prayed for us, and when we did attend, we felt unconditionally loved and accepted.

Though the last thing I felt like doing was rehashing my firing, this was not the time to become isolated. There were people in our former church, we discovered, who loved us and were hurt by my termination. They wanted to care for us, but they needed our permission to do so. We initiated contact with them and accepted their approaches toward us.

In the congregation I served, two other men had recently lost their jobs, and so I met regularly with them for mutual support and encouragement. When one of them found a new job, his success bolstered our confidence that we, too, would see God provide.

During the final weeks of the battle at our church, I had decided to leave pastoral ministry after my resignation. I concluded that "no job is worth this."

My wife described best what I was feeling: "It feels as though our lives have been vandalized."

It was like someone had crept into our lives, stealing our most precious possessions and damaging our values. Our trust in Christians evaporated, as did our love for giving and serving. Considering another church was impossible; we simply had nothing left to give.

In the weeks that followed my termination, however, the Lord challenged that conclusion. The first person he used was a seminary professor I happened to see. He mentioned he had heard the news of my termination. After consoling me for a few minutes, he said, "I hope you won't leave the pastorate; the church needs pastors like you."

"Perhaps you don't understand what we've been through—all the pressures and demands of church ministry," I replied. "It's different than teaching in a seminary where everyone professes a significant measure of spiritual maturity.

"No job or ministry is worth all the hassle and heartache I have experienced the past year," I continued. "There has to be another acceptable way for me to serve the Lord other than pastoring a local church."

Time and again, however, the professor's message was reiterated in different words from a variety of people who knew me well and had observed my ministry over the years. Talking with others familiar with my ministry refocused my calling. I had to overcome my fear of asking them for candid evaluations of my gifts, abilities, effectiveness, and calling.

Personality, temperament, and vocational testing were also helpful. My wife and I received this help at the retreat we attended in southwestern Colorado.

A probing question from a friend also aided my reevaluation. "What would you do for a living and a ministry," he asked, "if you knew God would grant you the ability to do it and bless you with success?"

Each time I answered that question, being a pastor topped my list. The more time passed, the more I regained my perspective on the call God had placed on my life to serve as a pastor. Six months after my termination, I joined the staff as associate pastor at the church we were attending.

When I left the home of the couple who had lost their jobs, the wisdom I offered that evening was academic and untried. But not anymore. Today my life is forever changed. Unemployment, I've discovered, can be redeemed by God, helping one refocus on the most precious element of our relationship: God's faithfulness.

Church conflict, I've come to realize, may be the most effective tool God has to shape our character. That is the thesis of this book. Both in the specific instance of my job termination and in the day-to-day conflict of pastoral ministry, I've discovered that God has changed me. I wouldn't have chosen such a route, but the frustration and hurt and loneliness of conflict have been used by God to develop my soul.

2

PLAYING HURT

RECENTLY I READ ABOUT a professional hockey player who is a star of the NHL team in the metro area near where I live. The measure of this man's stature as a hockey player was not his salary, number of goals scored, or minutes on the ice. Rather, the local sportswriter nominated him for greatness because of his ability to "play hurt."

Consider the symptoms of this athlete after receiving a hard check in the first period of play in a recent hockey game: He couldn't take a deep breath, he had bad bruises on his torso, and his shoulder and rib cage felt as though they had been through a meat grinder. His own description of his injuries made me cringe: "I couldn't breathe. It was lucky my head didn't land in the boards. I would have been dead, almost."

He was finished for the rest of that game.

Now consider the prognosis for this athlete: he was expected to return to the lineup after missing one game. Two, at most. To athletes, playing hurt is a badge of honor, reflecting the measure of their inner drive. The team needs them. They have to compete in the event. The work has to go on.

That's also true in ministry. Sometimes we just have to play hurt. In fact, we *often* have to play hurt. Some days I think this is what pastoral work is all about. Church conflicts leave scars from which some never fully recover. A battered soul doesn't heal quickly, yet most of us have to put food on the table—every day we go to the work that causes us pain. To stay in pastoral work means to play hurt in pastoral work.

We are often called to preach, pray, teach, visit, counsel, marry, and bury with wounded hearts.

A close friend is a retired pastor who is still going strong in his early eighties. He and I often talk about ministry, the good and the bad of it. One of his statements has stayed with me: he says that as he looks over his years in ministry and evaluates it quantitatively, the good far outweighs the bad. But he goes on: he says that when he does that same evaluation from a qualitative perspective, the good isn't that far ahead of the bad. Still, he says he keeps pressing on because he lays hold of the hope expressed by the apostle Paul that in light of eternity, our "troubles are achieving for us an eternal glory that far outweighs them all" (2 Cor. 4:17).

In my reading of the Bible, I'm often struck with the seemingly unfair advantage I have over the saints of Scripture. When I read stories about Noah, Abraham, Joseph, David, Job, and a host of others, I know the end of the story. Those who lived the stories, of course, didn't have that perspective. They were unsure of the destination while in the midst of the journey. They didn't know what God would bring out of it.

That is how we live our lives. We don't know the details of the end of our stories either. We are called upon to live faithfully without knowing how our story will conclude. Applied to ministry, we are called to play hurt without knowing when or if we will feel better.

Why it's so hard

Over the years I've mentored dozens of young people heading into the pastorate or other vocational ministry. It's not uncommon for me to hear later from them, once they've spent some time in ministry: "I can't take any more of this. Why didn't you tell me that life in the ministry could be so brutal?"

As I listen to their questions and their uncertainties about their calling, I often ask them a question I have posed to myself countless times: "Do you ever wonder why doesn't God do a better job of taking care of us in ministry?"

Surprised I would even ask such a question, they usually answer, "Yes, how'd you know? I didn't think anyone else ever asked that!"

If I were in God's place, doing His job for a time, I'd make sure I provided special care and protection for those on the front lines of ministry. But God doesn't seem to do that. There don't seem to be many breaks for vocational ministers. Sometimes the hurt seems unbearable.

Not every pastor reading my words will be able to say, "I've been through the conflict and have emerged better rather than bitter, healed through the hurt." There are times when healing, a word that defies definition, seems far away. At times I've wondered if I'll ever feel whole again. I have no pious platitudes.

I have a friend whom I mentored during his seminary years. We've stayed in touch through the fifteen years since he graduated and accepted his first pastorate. In his current church, he often says to me, "I feel so stuck here. These people don't want to move ahead; they want only to take what they need and then demand more. They want so much, pay so little, and then kick me when I'm down. I feel used and abused by them, but God doesn't seem to do anything about it."

My friend might read a book like this and ask, "What do you do with the wounds that never heal? Just about the time they scab over, someone comes along and rips off the scab." I've heard my friend paraphrase the words of Job so often, I have it memorized: "As the sparks fly upward, so is the pastor destined for use and abuse."

By the grace of God, I have found healing from and hope beyond church conflict, but this has come in developing a theology of church conflict. It hasn't eliminated the pain, but it has helped me press ahead when in the midst of it.

All-sufficient grace

The apostle Paul learned that in his weakness God's strength was manifest. God didn't take the thorn away. Instead God offered Paul the assurance that "My grace is sufficient for you, for my power is made perfect in weakness" (2 Cor. 12:9). Our hope is not so much the removal of our thorn but divine strength at the very time we need it. That's not much comfort on the one hand—I want relief from the incessant criticism—but on the other, the promise of strength from God means the world.

Another student I mentored some years ago confided in me that he feared standing up to preach in his church because of how angry and hurt he felt. He worried he would say something he would regret. Yet to his amazement, he discovered that while he struggled with anger and resentment, God seemed to continue to speak a clear and powerful message to the congregation each Sunday. My friend wondered how that could be, when he believed he was delivering many of those messages in the weakness of his flesh.

He discovered the power of Christ still rested on him even in weakness. I don't think God was excusing my friend's resentment or his inability to forgive his enemies or whatever his part in the conflict was, but God's grace was still operative in his life. As my friend was faithful to the preaching task, God was faithful to his Word.

I find more encouragement in reading about the

woes of the apostle Paul than perhaps about any other biblical character. His words and example help me keep going. Paul recognized the value of the message of the gospel that had been entrusted to him as a bondslave of Jesus Christ. He acknowledged that he himself was weak and frail and not up to the task. Out of that realization he wrote that "we have this treasure in jars of clay to show that this all-surpassing power is from God and not from us. We are hard pressed on every side, but not crushed; perplexed, but not in despair; persecuted, but not abandoned; struck down, but not destroyed. We always carry around in our body the death of Jesus, so that the life of Jesus may also be revealed in our body" (2 Cor. 4:7–10).

Though conflict rips out our hearts, God gives us his power to do his work. That strips us of pride and self-sufficiency—there are times when I press forward in my service to him out of total weakness, moving solely on God's power. Paul seems to indicate that is the norm rather than the exception: "We always carry around in our body the death of Jesus. . . . For we who are alive are always being given over to death for Jesus' sake, so that his life may be revealed in our mortal body" (2 Cor. 4:10–11). With Christ we are never devoid of hope, never left to our own strength. God never abandons us. Our weakness, wounds, and brokenness are opportunities to experience Christ's power and presence through us.

In my early years of pastoral ministry, I experienced this in a way I've never forgotten. I was serving overseas in an international church and was buffeted by repeated struggles with a young couple who was critical of me and negative about our church. I grew fearful of even seeing them on Sunday mornings. It seemed nothing measured up to their expectations.

At the suggestion of a friend in the church, a lay-leader and I scheduled a visit with this couple in their home on a Tuesday morning. As I traveled by tram across town to their apartment, I was nagged by anxiety and began to regret setting up the meeting. Hoping God would confirm my second-guessing and allow me to turn back, I opened my Bible as the tram noisily wound its way through the narrow streets toward my dreaded destination.

Two stops before mine I read, "Fear not, for I have redeemed you; I have summoned you by name; you are mine. When you pass through the waters, I will be with you; and when you pass through the rivers, they will not sweep over you.... For I am the Lord, your God, the Holy One of Israel, your Savior" (Isa. 43:1–3). At that moment I felt God's presence, as if his power was not only within me but around me.

That day my relationship with that couple began to turn around. Over the next four months, we experienced a renewed friendship and partnership in ministry.

Suffering identity

I remember as though it were this morning the first time I read Paul's startling words in Philippians

3:10–11: "I want to know Christ and the power of his resurrection and the fellowship of sharing in his sufferings, becoming like him in his death, and so, somehow, to attain to the resurrection from the dead."

How could Paul honestly write that?

I was a college student when I felt the joy of serving Christ; I certainly wasn't interested in knowing much about suffering. Two decades later my wife and I sat together at a Good Friday service in the church we were attending at the time. I had recently resigned from the church where I had been pastor. I was out of the pastorate. Suzanne and I were still in shock from the pain and disillusionment of the past two years.

Worshiping in that Good Friday service, I suddenly began to understand the previously confounding words of the apostle Paul. Out of my suffering for the sake of Christ came a deeper understanding of the suffering he endured to accomplish my salvation. I couldn't escape the thought that if Jesus had suffered that much for me, didn't he have the right to ask me to share in that suffering?

I arrived at a deeper understanding of God's love for me—God had given absolutely everything to bring me into his family. In light of that, I could endure seasons of suffering, knowing that is part of establishing Christ as the Lord of my life.

Learning to trust and obey

One final truth from God's Word that has sustained me through conflict, through times of playing hurt, is that even Jesus, God's Son, "learned obedience from what he suffered" (Heb. 5:8). Jesus was not following a script. He fully lived his life, choosing obedience at every turn. The Gospels record how some of his choices resulted in suffering, even for the Son of God. But it was from that suffering—playing hurt—that Jesus learned more about continued obedience to the will of his Father.

I was struck by that truth in the life of Gladys Aylward, missionary to China during and after World War II. Gladys's ministry in China was chronicled in the film "The Inn of the Sixth Happiness." She suffered terribly during her journey across the mountains of China in order to take a hundred orphans to safety in Sian in Shensi. Ranging in age from four to fifteen years old, these children were saved because of Gladys's faithful obedience to God.

But it was not without cost.

When Gladys arrived in Sian with the children, she was gravely ill and almost delirious. She suffered internal injuries from a beating by the Japanese invaders in the mission compound at Tsechow. In addition, she suffered from relapsing fever, typhus, pneumonia, malnutrition, shock, and fatigue.

Through her ordeal, Gladys learned to choose Christ over anything else life had to offer—so much so that when the man she loved, Colonel Linnan, came to visit her in Sian as she was recovering and asked her to marry him, she declined. In her heart she knew she could not marry him and continue the work

God had for her among the children of China. Out of her obedience to God, she said good-bye to Linnan at the Sian train station, and they never met again. Gladys continued serving God faithfully in China and England until her death in 1970.

Through our suffering in ministry, God wants us to increase our maturity in Christ. Today I'm better able to trust God and obey him because of my painful experiences. Harsh criticism I've received in the past has taught me to listen longer and respond with a gentler answer to my critics today. From suffering I learn more about obedience.

Recently a man in our church opined in a meeting that I had lied to the congregation in a recent sermon. There was a time when he wouldn't have finished his sentence before I would have challenged what he said and set him straight. But sometimes there is wisdom in remaining silent before accusers. I never had a chance to respond to his accusations. One after another, people stood up and confronted his erroneous statements and challenged his harsh indictments. His response after being rebutted was, "I guess I jumped to unwarranted conclusions and was harsh in my judgments."

Then, turning to me, he said, "I'm sorry for what I said."

I'm learning more about what it means to allow God to be my defender, rather than jumping to my own defense. It's tough to trust God with that, but doing so is part of my obedience in allowing him to work out his plan in and through my life.

Playing hurt in pastoral work is no one's idea of fun. Somehow, through pain and perseverance, we can discover the truth Paul expressed so eloquently: "We also rejoice in our sufferings, because we know that suffering produces perseverance; perseverance, character; and character, hope. And hope does not disappoint us, because God has poured out his love into our hearts by the Holy Spirit, whom he has given us" (Rom. 5:3–5).

3

KEEPING ENEMIES CLOSE

I WAS IN MY NEW PASTORATE for less than three months when one of the founding laymen took me to lunch.

"It seems to me," he started out, "and I've confirmed this with a number of other key people in the church, that you may not be the right person for this job after all." He pointed to a couple of insignificant (at least to me) changes I had made in the worship service and how that had offended some people involved in our music program.

"In fact," he warned, "there are a growing number of people who just plain don't like you or where you're leading the church. I'm not sure those people will remain in the church if you stay."

This is yet another anecdote from the story I told in chapter 1. Perhaps it was a harbinger of what was to come. I certainly didn't realize it at the time. After my forced exit, I realized that I had either ignored or avoided or didn't know about a key role of leadership: As a pastor, I must maintain healthy relationships with all the people in the church, even those with whom that is difficult. Put bluntly, I must shepherd people who don't like me—and those I don't really like.

That is an enormous challenge, especially when you're feeling beat up, insecure, and ready to throw in the towel. Another challenge may be the simple admission that, truth be told, we don't like certain people in the church. We want to believe we love all of God's children.

But it seems that it's normal for every church to have a couple people who are tough to like and, consequently, tough to pastor. Not to care for those who persecute us, though, only invites trouble down the road. Our instincts drive us to avoid feeling uncomfortable, but that drive can cripple our effectiveness as leaders.

Nowhere in Scripture am I instructed to shepherd only the agreeable sheep.

Resist what comes naturally

In ministry, doing what comes naturally is often the best approach. At the bedside of a hospital patient, with families at a funeral, or when sharing the gospel with a nonbeliever, my pastoral instincts usually guide me in the right direction. However, that's not true when it comes to pastoring difficult people. One of my natural responses is to distance myself from difficult people.

Therefore, I've had to learn to make it a point to seek out difficult people and spend a few moments talking together with them.

Recently a woman in our church let it be known that, in her opinion, I had acted out of anger and harshness. She voiced her criticism after she had sent me a letter apologizing for her role in the issue and commending me for the way I had handled it!

When I saw her at a community event a few days later, she walked past me without saying more than "Hello." I could have let it pass and rationalized that her coldness was her problem. In such situations, I typically think, *She'll get over it.* I wanted to ignore her, let her stew, and wait for her to come to me.

Instead, I decided not to do what comes naturally. I practically had to chase her down the hallway. When I caught up with her, I didn't confront her about her actions or anger toward me; I engaged her in friendly conversation to make sure she knew I wanted to connect with her.

It was amazing what those two minutes did. We ended up laughing about something one of her children had said that week. She hugged me as I left and gave me a look that communicated, "Thanks for talking to me; I needed that."

Even if our contact with the person doesn't solve the problem, it builds a bridge rather than a wall. There is something positive and healing about face-to-face contact with people at odds with us.

Invite talk about sensitive subjects

The next time I saw this woman, we were able to talk with more ease, so I broached the subject of our conflict. My purpose wasn't to make a point or add another thought about the subject. I simply said, "I've been wondering how you are processing your frustration. I want you to know that I care."

This second contact was easier for both of us, and it communicated to her that we could talk about the issue. The subject didn't need to be avoided. It's important to let people know that even subjects of conflict can be discussed; they don't have to end the relationship.

I've had ongoing differences with one couple over the style of our worship service. I've met with them on a couple of occasions to talk specifically about the issue. We continue to disagree. We see each other regularly, and sometimes when we are talking about something unrelated to worship, I will intentionally bring the subject into our conversation. I might casually ask, "I've been wondering if you have noticed any positive changes in the worship services lately?" Or, "Did you enjoy the extra hymns we sang today?"

I'm not trying to stir up controversy; I simply want them to know it's okay to talk about something we disagree on. We can disagree and still work together.

Keep private battles private

One of my bigger relational mistakes came at a church meeting. One person had battled me repeatedly about my emphasis on evangelism. At a business meeting the subject of evangelism came up, and several people expressed their excitement about how the church was finally reaching out.

I jumped at the opportunity to say, "Of course, there are some in the church who tell me that we are losing more people than we are gaining because of this strong focus on evangelism."

Almost everyone recognized that I was referring to the "no evangelism" proponent. The majority of the people supported our evangelism philosophy. It was clear my critic was part of a shrinking minority. I had scored a major victory on that issue, and a public one at that—or so I thought.

Ultimately, the statement came back to haunt me. Just as a negative political ad campaign can generate sympathy for the opponent, so too can a public attack against someone in the church. The week following, I heard comments like, "I don't think it was fair to say what you did about Ed. He can't be as opposed to evangelism as you implied."

Someone else said, "That wasn't appropriate to raise an issue about Ed's position when he was not present to respond."

I could support every statement I had made about Ed's opposition to evangelism. That didn't seem to matter. Even though people didn't agree with his position, they disagreed even more with my public attack of him.

The moral is some things are best left unsaid—an obvious principle that gets ignored or overlooked when the heat gets turned up. Don't take private battles public. That's true in a board meeting or in the pulpit or in a conversation with someone who is in the "doesn't need to know" category.

Practice kindness

A bumper sticker adorns the bumpers of numerous cars in my community. It reads: *Practice random acts of kindness and senseless acts of beauty.* It's a good reminder of one of the most helpful lessons I've learned about pastoring people I find difficult to love.

I look for opportunities to be nice to them. It is amazing what acts of kindness can do to build bridges to people. A man in a former church let me know every time I failed to fulfill some expectation of his. Whether returning a phone call within his prescribed time limit, reciprocating a lunch invitation, or giving him an equal number of compliments to the ones he gave me, he seemed to keep score in a way that made me the perpetual loser.

I found him increasingly difficult to be around. After the Lord convicted me of my attitude, I began to look for ways to show him kindness.

I stopped him after church one Sunday and said, "I was wondering if you might be available this next week to help me work on my fly-fishing." He was an avid fly-fisherman, and I could hardly catch a weed in a stream. In the weeks after our outing, he often referred to our fishing lesson in conversations with me and others.

Fishing on my own sometime later, I finally caught a fish big enough to keep. On the way home, I stopped by my "instructor's" house and presented him with my first big catch as a gift for helping me learn to fly-fish.

Another time, I invited him to go skiing, and he asked me to show him how to canoe. On some outings, we talked about his need to keep score of people's behavior to make himself the winner. He eventually admitted this was negatively affecting his wife and his oldest son. I offered some help on how to deal with it.

When best efforts fall short

Of course, no approach to dealing with difficult people will be successful with all people all the time. In Romans 12:18, the apostle Paul said, "If it is possible, as far as it depends on you, live at peace with everyone." Paul recognized that not everyone will want to live at peace with us.

What do we do when our best efforts still come up short?

In a former church, one lady never seemed fully satisfied with anything I did. Seldom would she tell me directly of her displeasure; I usually heard it through an intermediary source.

I met with her and told her, "I'm unable to live up

to your standards of performance and expectations for my ministry. I feel as though I can't please you." I told her that since I couldn't, I was going to stop trying.

Of course, she assured me I didn't have to please her.

I responded, "So you won't mind if I no longer concern myself with pleasing you with every action and decision?"

She said she wouldn't. That took the pressure off and diffused some of her constant complaining. I shared with our elders my conversation with this woman so that if her carping continued, they could address the issue with her directly and decisively.

Sometimes, of course, people decide they can no longer be a part of my life or ministry and leave the church. I've learned even here to open the door of communication as much as possible.

One couple told me they could no longer support my ministry or sit under my preaching. My natural response was to let them leave and not to contact them. Instead, I picked up the phone and asked if I could stop by for a brief visit. They reluctantly agreed.

When we met I told them I was not there to talk them out of their decision. I asked if there were specific incidents where I had wronged or offended them personally. I wanted to apologize if there were. They said the issue was more a difference in philosophy and direction, so they decided it was best to find another church. I thanked them for their years of ministry at our church and invited them back anytime. Before I left I asked if I could pray with them.

As I walked toward the door, the wife took my hand and said, "I was surprised you wanted to visit us, but I'm glad you did. Now when I see you at the supermarket, I won't have to avoid talking to you." The door of communication was still open. They may not come back to the church, but at least they didn't leave with a bitter spirit.

Not only are these approaches helpful in building good relationships in general, they yield personal growth in my relationship with Christ. The more I seek to love difficult people, the more God uses them to refine me into the image of Christ. After all, learning to love people is one of the ways we become like Christ. Perhaps it's the main instrument for pastors in that process.

Staying close to our enemies will usually open doors of ministry beyond what we imagined. That ought to motivate us to care for even the most difficult saints.

4

RESISTING THE URGE TO STRIKE BACK

I HAD JUST RECEIVED a scathing letter from a couple unhappy about a situation in the youth department. Their response was carnal; they certainly didn't understand the whole situation. I hadn't yet been able to meet with them.

When I stepped up to preach that Sunday morning, I felt ungracious and carried a grudge. During my introduction, I made some ad-lib quips that gave everyone a chuckle—everyone except the couple who had sent the letter. While the congregation held their sides in laughter, this couple sat stoically, second row, center section, arms folded, eyes staring through me.

By the time I finished the sermon (with no more humor), I felt physically sick and spiritually wasted. My unforgiveness was quickly growing into bitterness and resentment—the twin temptations of church conflict. Most pastors have preached that temptation isn't sin but that giving in to the temptation is. Yet, at least for me, it's a temptation hard to resist. The issue of forgiveness is a character issue, and my tendency not to forgive when I've been wronged has forced me to think clearly about the steps I need to take to restore my relationship with God and the offender.

Recognize my weak spots

Most people tend to be sensitive where they've been battered numerous times. The criticism leveled at me by the family angry about the youth ministry event was only one in a series of skirmishes with them. Their attitude, devoid of grace, was the final straw for me. I felt they had no interest in giving anyone the benefit of the doubt.

Perhaps because some of my worst conflicts in ministry have involved people who I felt lacked grace and understanding, I tend to react with anger in such situations. I'm quickly set off by people who excel in fault-finding.

As I've learned to recognize my weak spots, I've found I am better able to control my responses. My challenge is to receive from the Holy Spirit grace and forgiveness for these saints rather than fight back in anger, unforgiveness, and bitterness.

Resist my first impulse

When I read of a person who conceals a gun in his coat pocket to get even with a boss who treated him wrongly, or someone who bombs a building full of innocent citizens, I often think, *How could someone do such a thing? Normal people just don't react like that.*

But I've had all kinds of evil thoughts about settling the score with people who I felt had wronged me. Perhaps that's the next move toward forgiveness—recognizing that, if given the right circumstances, I could exact a vicious retribution. In fact, if I don't forgive someone, I can begin to fantasize about ways to get even.

After a devastating disagreement with a church family who had opposed me on nearly every issue and subject, I thought, *If God isn't going to bring swift judgment, I could offer some assistance.*

I thought about alerting the IRS to their tax improprieties I happened to know about. Or I could become a nocturnal nuisance by driving by their house with my radio blaring, horn honking, and high-beams shining in their windows.

When I shared these dastardly secret thoughts with a friend, he looked at me in astonishment. "Could you really do those things to them?"

I said, "Sure, just like anyone could who yields to the temptation to get revenge instead of tackling the challenge of forgiveness."

I am reminded of the observation James Broderick made of Pope Paul IV: "He never forgot such offenses, which was one of his fundamental weaknesses. He might bury the hatchet for a time, but he gave the impression of always carefully marking the spot."

I avoid that only by curtailing any fantasies of revenge.

Admit my guilt

In Deuteronomy 32:35, God instructed the people through Moses: "It is mine to avenge; I will repay. In due time their foot will slip; their day of disaster is near and their doom rushes upon them."

My obsessing about revenge is an attempt to participate in God's judgment. That only aggravates the conflict, exacerbates the memory of it, and causes more pain. It's like having one of the guilty parties in a contractual dispute participate in the trial and sentencing of the other party. Justice cannot be served by one guilty party judging the other.

The fact that I am also often guilty, that I haven't been perfectly righteous in my actions, can be hard to accept. In many instances, there are two guilty parties in conflict. Therefore, I cannot have any part in repaying the wrong. I wonder how many reconciliation opportunities have broken down because both parties came together prepared to forgive but were unprepared to be forgiven. John Oglethorpe, a friend of John Wesley, allegedly told Wesley, "I never forgive."

Mr. Wesley wisely replied, "Then, sir, I hope that you never sin."

Avoid pulpit revenge

I have found that delaying forgiveness can lead me to abuse the public ministry of preaching. I once used a critical letter I received to illustrate how wrong it is to criticize someone when you don't know all the facts. During the sermon I read a portion of the letter, which made accusations and drew conclusions based on misinformation. Then I set the record straight for the congregation by describing the facts of the situation. Of course, the facts demonstrated how my critics had jumped to the wrong conclusion and had been at fault in their criticism.

The congregation seemed to sympathize with me and saw my accuser as a careless and negative antagonist. I had illustrated a biblical point and silenced my opponent at the same time.

The next week I received a second letter from this man stating that he and his family were leaving the church and asking me not to call or contact them. While I had carefully protected their identity in the sermon illustration, they knew to whom I was referring. I had left them no way out but to leave.

No matter how wronged I may have felt, and no matter how strong the temptation, the public forum was and is not the place to confront a critic. It gives me a lopsided advantage that too often results in a biased presentation of my side of the story without an opportunity for a fair rebuttal.

I've discovered the best way to defend against this temptation is to offer forgiveness privately.

Forgive one at a time

I wish I could say I've found the formula for forgiveness that works the first time, every time. I haven't. Forgiveness isn't something I can do once, then it's all over. The length of the forgiveness process is usually proportionate to the severity of the pain. Forgiveness is more like writing a book than writing a letter. When I write a letter, I put my thoughts on paper, sign it, seal the envelope, and send it. Writing a book involves what seems an endless cycle of writing and rewriting.

I can usually handle minor conflicts quickly, in the spirit of 1 Peter 4:8: "Above all, love each other deeply, because love covers over a multitude of sins." But when the offense is severe, the process of forgiveness can be equally severe. Following the most difficult experience I've had in ministry—being terminated—I learned more about the process of forgiveness than I wanted to know. The entire process took close to two years. It seemed like my forgiveness was complete within a few months after I left that ministry. I brought the incident to the Lord in prayer and told him I wanted to forgive those whom I felt were responsible. I even listed them by name. Forgiveness seemed to release me.

But a couple of weeks later, I ran into one of the opposition leaders at a local restaurant. After my friend and I finished our breakfast, we stopped by this person's table for a brief but cordial chat. As we left the restaurant, my friend remarked, "Boy, you sure seemed at ease talking with Steve. I guess you've been able to put all of that stuff from the church behind you."

I mumbled, "Yeah, that's old business now; it's time to move ahead." But for the rest of the day, every time I had an idle minute, Steve's name, face, and actions came rushing to the forefront of my mind. I couldn't get rid of my thoughts. That old resentment seemed as real and powerful as ever—a shocking blow to my spiritual equilibrium.

I thought I had forgiven those in that debacle. Why was I reacting like this?

"Lord, isn't it enough to put that whole mess in a package, tie it up tightly, and then write 'forgiven' across it?"

Evidently not. I still had to forgive each of the eight individuals in the conflict. While thinking I could forgive in one composite act, I discovered I would have to forgive one by one.

The process lasted many more months. Each time I fantasized about one person, I identified clearly what I was feeling toward the specific person God brought to mind. Sometimes that took a few days to think through thoroughly. But finally I was able to write down my feelings as well as identify the reasons behind them. I discovered that the simple act of praying for someone, even when it felt hollow and rehearsed, had a way of opening my heart toward that person.

God was creative in showing me the next person I needed to forgive. I was in the supermarket looking for toothpaste and shaving cream, when out of the corner of my eye I saw another couple who had contributed to my termination. My reaction was to hide among the vegetable displays. Too late. I heard that familiar drawl, "Well, hi there, Gary." After several short sentences, we parted.

I knew immediately the next person whom I needed to forgive.

Speak about the person to others

One technique that helped me forgive was to speak about the person who had wronged me in conversations with others.

I remember talking about one antagonist to a friend who knew him; that way, I put myself in a position that forced me to speak kindly of him. But I discovered that whether or not the person I conversed with knew the person I needed to forgive was irrelevant. By speaking positively about someone, I felt pushed toward reconciliation; the positive words forming on my lips began to work on the feelings in my heart. The ease of those words also became a gauge of my forgiveness—the easier they flowed, the further along I discovered I was in the forgiveness process.

Take them to the Lord in prayer

A final step that helped me to forgive was to gather my thoughts and feelings and take them to the Lord. Sometimes I would write them on paper and read them to God in prayer. Other times I recited them to God directly from my thoughts. Reciting negative thoughts and feelings to the Lord allowed me to ask God to forgive me for my sin. I was then able, with his help, to move forward to offer forgiveness to others.

This protracted experience of forgiveness taught me how much God's forgiveness of me enables my forgiveness of others.

There's a story about a traveler making his way with a guide through the jungles of Burma. They came to a wide but shallow river and waded through it to the other side. When the traveler came out of the river, numerous leeches had attached to his torso and legs. His first instinct was to grab them and pull them off.

This guide stopped him, warning that pulling the leeches off would only leave tiny pieces of them under the skin. Eventually, infection would set in.

The best way to rid the body of the leeches, the guide advised, was to bathe in a warm balsam bath for several minutes. This would soak the leeches, and soon they would release their hold on the man's body.

When I've been significantly injured by another person, I cannot simply yank the injury from my soul and expect that all bitterness, malice, and emotion will be gone. Resentment still hides under the surface. The only way to become truly free of the offense and to forgive others is to bathe in the soothing bath of God's forgiveness of me. When I finally fathom the extent of God's love in Jesus Christ, forgiveness of others is a natural outflow.

5

PREACHING THROUGH CONTROVERSY

THIS PAST SUMMER MY FAMILY ATTENDED a Christian family conference hosted by the radio ministry of a well-known American pastor. Over the years I have enjoyed listening to him preach countless sermons, both in person and by audiotape. I have profited spiritually from his exposition of the Scriptures.

During one message at the conference, he illustrated from his life. That was no surprise, for it was fairly common for him to insert personal anecdotes into his sermons. Frequently these stories were of the rubber-meets-the-road variety of family-life events. This, however, was different. A hush came over the audience as he told his story.

The story was about a soul-wrenching conflict that had affected his entire family. But it wasn't the details of the story that gripped me—in fact, the details were purposely vague because of the intensely personal nature of the pain. The impact came not from what he said, but from what he was unable to say.

His story did not have a conclusion; he and his family were still in the midst of the struggle. As he ended the illustration, he said, "I wish that I could close this story by telling you that everything has been taken care of and we have seen the faithfulness of the Lord's healing touch. But I can't, because we haven't. We're still hurting and waiting to see how God will work all of this out. And so we wait ... and we wait ... and we continue to wait."

That was a powerful reminder of the peculiar challenge pastors often face preaching the great promises of God during times when we ourselves are still waiting for those promises to be fulfilled. Sometimes we bear the pain and heartache of conflict while holding forth in our preaching the hope we have in God. Perhaps this challenge is never greater than when we have to preach to those who have perpetrated pain in our lives. Speaking the truths of God to people we know are plotting to undo us is daunting. I've found it troubling to preach when I know that one person in the congregation doesn't like me.

How do we preach through pain, to people we may not like and who may not think much of us? How do we bring a message from God while trying to push down all the unresolved hurt and anger? Although I've been preaching for more than twenty years, I'm still trying to fully answer those questions. The conclusions I've drawn in this chapter are certainly tentative at best. For with each new conflict, I learn more about what it means to proclaim the truths of God amid the brokenness of life.

Unfulfilled promise

One challenge of the Old Testament saints was to proclaim the promises of God and to exemplify a steadfast faith when they themselves had not received what was promised. In his conclusion to the great faith chapter (Heb. 11), the author surprises his readers by announcing that the heroes of their faith died without receiving the total fulfillment of God's promises:

> And what more shall I say? I do not have time to tell about Gideon, Barak, Samson, Jephthah, David, Samuel and the prophets, who through faith conquered kingdoms, administered justice, and gained what was promised; who shut the mouths of lions, quenched the fury of the flames, and escaped the edge of the sword; whose weakness was turned to strength; and who became powerful in battle and routed foreign armies. Women received back their dead, raised to life again. Others were tortured and refused to be released, so that they might gain a better resurrection. Some faced jeers and flogging, while still others were chained and put in prison. They were stoned; they were sawed in two; they were put to death by the sword. They went about in sheepskins and goatskins, destitute, per-

secuted and mistreated—the world was not worthy of them. They wandered in deserts and mountains, and in caves and holes in the ground. These were all commended for their faith, yet none of them received what had been promised. God had planned something better for us so that only together with us would they be made perfect. (vv. 32–40)

Yet these leaders still proclaimed God's promises to a needy nation. I suspect that is what God calls pastors to do. In the midst of conflict that has yet to be resolved, we must hold forth the promises of God. For it's the promises themselves, not only their fulfillment, that call forth faith.

When I preach during a period of conflict, I ask myself what specific promises of God would be relevant to that situation. I once had a man in the church accuse me of being greedy because I asked the budget committee for a much-deserved (and long-delayed) salary increase for the staff. He didn't seem to understand there was a spiritual principle of sowing and reaping at play in how the church treated its staff. In his mind, my asking for a raise for the staff was an expression of greed rather than generosity. After a particularly harsh criticism that he leveled at me during a budget meeting, I went home angry and hurt. I wrestled the rest of the week with having to stand before the congregation on Sunday and preach grace when I felt like dispensing God's wrath.

Finally, on Saturday morning I sat down and began to list the promises of God that were applicable to the situation. On a piece of paper I wrote:

> My God shall supply all your need. (Phil. 4:19 KJV)
>
> I have learned to be content whatever the circumstances. (Phil. 4:11)
>
> The God of all grace . . . will himself restore you and make you strong. (1 Pet. 5:10)
>
> Seek first his kingdom and his righteousness, and all these things will be given to you as well. (Matt. 6:33)
>
> Do not worry about tomorrow, for tomorrow will worry about itself. (Matt. 6:34)

I had memorized most of these as a child in Sunday school. Throughout my life God had fulfilled them time and again. But not this time—at least not yet. But the process of writing down these promises, though not yet fulfilled, helped me release my disappointment and hostility. I realized the issue was in God's hands; rereading God's promises helped me to hand back the responsibility to him.

Softened hearts

When the apostle Paul confronted his accusers in Acts 24, he used the method of preaching. Before the

Roman governor Felix, Paul's response to the prosecuting lawyer Tertullus was in the form of a sermon. So effective was his rejoinder that Tertullus was silenced and Governor Felix was moved to give Paul a greater measure of freedom even while he was still under guard.

Again in Acts 26, Paul responded to his accusers with a sermon before King Agrippa. Paul spoke in the power of the Holy Spirit, intending to convince Agrippa to become a Christian. Although that did not happen, God used Paul's proclamation to convince Agrippa of the apostle's innocence.

Preaching in the midst of conflict can be a means for allowing the Holy Spirit to soften the hearts of adversaries. Certainly that is tricky, for preaching to confront adversaries requires skill and integrity. There is a fine line between authentically preaching biblical truth to accusers and using the sermon and the Bible to bludgeon them.

An issue arose in our church related to the growing number of youth coming to the services. Many of the young people had recently discovered a personal relationship with God through faith in Jesus Christ. To highlight what God was doing among the teens, we asked the youth ministry to lead the congregation in corporate worship one Sunday.

The youth jumped to the challenge with energy, creativity, and enthusiasm. The result was a moving worship experience for the entire church family. God enabled us to capture the hearts and minds of three generations simultaneously, bringing them together in worship in a unique way.

In light of that powerful encounter with God, I was surprised when I heard criticism about the way a number of the youth were dressed for the worship service. They said the young people's casual dress was disruptive to the work of the Holy Spirit and disrespectful to some of the adults in the church. The next couple of weeks I discussed the issue with the unhappy folks. It seemed I was getting nowhere, except that their vitriol was increasing and starting to be directed toward me. Likewise, the youth and their supporters were growing more vocal in their arguments. One woman told me in no uncertain terms, "If we have to make a choice between reverence for the Lord in worship and having our youth participate like that, then both the youth and you will lose!"

The stakes were higher than I thought. Rather than continue down the path of private dialogue, I decided to address the issue publicly. I was careful to direct my message to the issue before us rather than to the people in dissent. To do that I used the message of Acts 15 as the text and titled the sermon "Freedom Worth Fighting For." The point was that our spiritual freedom and liberty are core Christian values. I tried to show how from the Book of Acts onward, there have been constant attacks on the liberty Jesus Christ won for us on the Cross. Acts 15 says our relationship with God begins solely by grace through faith; the life that results is a life of liberty and freedom in Jesus Christ.

In my presentation, I addressed both groups, who glared at each other across the aisle. I showed how the Jerusalem Council's decision in Acts 15 makes it difficult to determine the condition of a person's heart toward God by looking at the style of her clothing or noticing the absence of shoes or socks from his feet. On the other hand, one's liberty not to wear shoes must never be exercised in a way that disregards or disdains the convictions of others. Rather, we must exercise our liberty in Christ with a spirit of sensitivity and concern for others in God's family.

The response to the sermon was more than I had asked God for.

The first person to catch me after the service was an older lady who had been in tears only weeks before after the youth service because of her distress over "the young people's disregard for the Lord's house." She took my hand and said, "I don't know if I can get used to people not wearing shoes in church, but now I see that it doesn't have anything to say about how much they love the Lord." Similar sentiments were voiced repeatedly that morning by people on both sides of the issue. I was again amazed at the power of God's Word to bring reconciliation.

Log in your eye

In conflict I can become too focused on intersecting the message of Scripture with the lives of those with whom I disagree. Doing so inhibits the impact Scripture has on my life.

Once I preached a sermon series on the epistle of James when there was a small-scale war of words going on in the church. Most of the loose talk was focused on differences of opinion concerning our building project.

As I planned the sermon series, I could hardly wait until I got to chapter 3. What James had to say about "taming the tongue" was just what many needed to hear! Finally the Sunday to preach that passage arrived. I prayed all week that the Lord would use the message to soften hardened hearts. I did my best to connect the message of James with the words that had been spoken by members of our congregation. For the most part, I felt God answered my prayers. After the sermon people acknowledged to me that the Lord had spoken to them that morning and that they intended to mend some fences that coming week.

On Tuesday afternoon at the men's fellowship group, I conveyed my excitement about how God had used Sunday's sermon to challenge people. A couple of men acknowledged that they, too, were thankful for the way the Lord had used my message. Then another man cleared his throat, looked me square in the face, and said, "Does that mean that you want to clear the air with us over some of the things you have said in recent weeks?"

I had no idea what he meant. I thought at first he was trying to catch me with his dry humor, so I retorted with an off-the-cuff quip.

"No, we're serious," he said. "As I listened to the message on Sunday I wondered if you were hearing what you were saying."

They had me. They talked straight to me, reminding me of statements I had made to them during the building conflict. Some of my comments had been gossipy and even slanderous. In the midst of preparing and delivering a sermon on taming the tongue, I had been deaf to the Spirit's voice about my own transgressions. I, too, needed to pay attention to James's message.

That incident reminded me about the importance of allowing my study and preaching to address me first. It's easy for preachers to study, prepare, and preach the holy truths of God to a congregation before addressing themselves. Phillip Brooks, the great nineteenth-century rector of Boston's Trinity Church, illustrated this peril with the analogy of a train conductor who comes to believe that he has been to all the places he announces to the passengers because of his long and loud heralding of the names of those places.

Allowing my preaching to address me first keeps me from using the sermon as a weapon. I keep a blank notepad on the corner of my desk during sermon study. Throughout the week, I ask the Holy Spirit to bring to my mind particular issues or areas of my life where the message I'm preparing applies. As these thoughts come to mind, I write them down so I can pray about them before God prior to concluding my study that morning. I'm constantly amazed at how thoroughly God applies to my life the truths I'm studying for Sunday. That helps me identify the log in my eye before I become obsessed with the speck in someone else's.

Needed cushion

A friend has been embroiled in conflict in his church for the past six months. So snarled is the situation that he is planning to offer his resignation within the next two weeks. When I talked with him this week, I asked him how he has been able to continue preaching every Sunday while his adversaries have maligned him and managed to gain the upper hand in the struggle splitting the church.

His response: "I've had a cushion between me and the congregation."

He explained that an elder in the church, a friend and mature Christian, has stood in the gap between pastor and congregation. My friend credits him with allowing him to vent his thoughts and emotions in a safe setting. That, my friend says, has kept him from leaking toxic resentment to the congregation through his preaching. He told me, "When I've unloaded my frustration during the week to my 'cushion,' I don't feel the burning need to do that in the Sunday sermon."

During my darkest days in ministry, I discovered

the value of such friends. A businessman, an oph-thalmologist, an engineer, and a scientist were the friends I turned to to vent my frustrations, ask my questions, and offer my solutions. They mostly listened, occasionally offered advice, but always provided strength and support.

At one low point I called one of these friends as a last straw. "Can I come by and bend your ear for a while this evening?" I asked.

"Come on over," he said, "the coffee will be brewed when you get here."

Ten minutes later I sat with him and his wife at their dining room table and told them I didn't think I had it in me to continue.

"Being a pastor requires constant giving," I said, "and I'm afraid I have nothing more to give to anyone. I have to get out before this thing kills me." Those were words I never thought I'd say. I wanted out, a feeling that was so foreign to me.

Through two pots of coffee, we talked into the night. Finally my friends convinced me that it was not time to throw in the towel. They said, "We will stand in the gap for you. You take the next two weeks off, and we will go before the elders and the church on your behalf and explain that you need some time away from the pressure."

Since my friend was also an elder, I knew his decision would be acceptable to the board. I also recognized that the congregation would be supportive. My concern was about the three families who led the opposition and held the power in the church. What would they do with this news that I was on the ropes? Would they somehow move in for the knockout punch?

My friends told me, "That is no longer your concern. You are now on two weeks leave. We want you to go skiing tomorrow and leave the church alone for a while."

Their boldness was convincing. Instead of resigning, I stopped worrying (at least for the next few months), and I went skiing with my wife the next day.

That sort of protection from friends prevented me from even more conflict—the kind that comes when you say things you shouldn't because you're so weary and beat up. They allowed me to direct my frustrations, questions, and even hostility, toward them rather than toward those instigating the strife.

I've had to learn to trust these people, and doing so has been worth it: when I lean on them, I find I am more spiritually ready to handle God's Word in an objective way. I tend not to allow my wounds to distort my preaching, and thus I don't misuse the ministry of the Word.

Preaching that comforts me

During church conflict, my preaching has comforted me. I know that sounds a little strange, but if I allow God to do his work in me prior to accomplishing his work through me, I can find healing in my preaching. Once I preached from Psalm 139 in the midst of intense conflict. As I prepared for Sunday, the moving lyrics of Psalm 139 brought me comfort; God was speaking directly to me. Never before had I experienced such intimacy with God, his thoughts becoming more and more precious to me. I felt reassured that God was in control, that everything would turn out as he had planned.

God's special ministry to me that week emboldened me to proclaim that same hope on Sunday. After the service, rather than the usual hustle toward the refreshment table, many people remained in their seats to continue listening to and talking with the Lord. A small group approached me and asked if they could pray with me there on the platform steps. We knelt and prayed and experienced a profound sense of God's presence. During a time when the waves of conflict were capsizing the church, Psalm 139 overwhelmed us with God himself:

> How precious to me are your thoughts, O God! How vast is the sum of them! Were I to count them, they would outnumber the grains of sand. When I awake, I am still with you. If only you would slay the wicked, O God! Away from me, you bloodthirsty men! They speak of you with evil intent; your adversaries misuse your name. Do I not hate those who hate you, O Lord, and abhor those who rise up against you? I have noth-

ing but hatred for them; I count them my enemies. Search me, O God, and know my heart; test me and know my anxious thoughts. See if there is any offensive way in me, and lead me in the way everlasting. (Psa. 139:17–24).

6

WHAT YOUR FAMILY NEEDS

I WAS IN MY SECOND YEAR of college when the pastor of my home church made a shocking announcement. I can still remember the aching feeling in my stomach as I sat in the congregational meeting on a Sunday afternoon and heard the pastor, whom I admired and loved, explain that his wife was having an affair with a man in the church.

That occurred at a time when such revelations were still rare and scandalous.

The congregation was stunned. No one knew what to say. No one knew how to respond to the need in his family and the brokenness of his heart. Later I heard that he left the church after that meeting and returned only to clean out his office and pack his books. He and his family left the church, moved from the city, and were never heard from again.

The pastor wasn't the only one in his family who was hurting, of course. In that congregational meeting, he told about the grief his wife had been feeling for more than a year. Much of her travail was the result of the conflict that had been going on in the church for months. She would come home from choir practice in tears, vowing never to go back again. I guess the conflict took its toll.

Her role in the conflict was primarily as a spectator, though her husband was at the epicenter of the controversy. Few folks offered her comfort or understanding, assuming that she and her family would somehow get through it on their own. They didn't, and I guess she found her solace in the arms of another.

Though I won't justify her behavior, I can empathize with her loneliness. When we left a church in the midst of conflict, my wife told me, "I would be eternally grateful to God if he would just let you leave the pastorate." During another time of turmoil, she confided, "If you got out of the pastorate, I would have no regrets. This life as a pastor's family is just too painful and lonely." At one of our lowest points, she told me, "I hate the church and wouldn't regret it for a minute if I never had to go back."

Church conflict can deeply wound a pastor's wife, sometimes irrevocably. (Since the majority of pastors' spouses are still women, I will refer in this chapter to wives rather than spouses.) She's hurting, her husband is hurting, and neither can help the other. Several years ago, after the worst church conflict in my ministry led to my resignation and immediate expulsion from the church, I was fortunate that a colleague offered me his friendship. During one of our times together, he asked, "How is Suzanne holding up through all of this?"

Tears came to my eyes because I knew she was hurting as much as I was, but I didn't know how to respond to her needs. When ministry is buffeted by conflict, the pastor's marriage can—and should—be a sheltering tree for both him and his wife. Even if there is disunity in the body of Christ, the pastoral couple can, with God's help, be united in their commitment to Christ and to each other.

But it's not easy for the pastor embroiled in conflict to come home and think about his wife's needs. The fact that God takes conflict and forges out of it our character is one of the key themes of this book, and that is no more true than in caring for our family. In the opening chapter, I discussed briefly how during the time of my forced exit from ministry, Suzanne and I guarded our family. In this chapter, however, I want to focus on the importance of making an effort to understand, acknowledge, and respect your wife's feelings.

Sting of betrayal

Pastors' wives form their own connections in a congregation, and when conflict tears at a ministry they can feel deeply betrayed by people they trusted. During one of our church battles, Suzanne had been meeting regularly with several women in the church. It was a group she enjoyed spending time with and trusted, and often they would discuss very personal issues about their lives. Suzanne felt she could confide in these friends about our situation. She spoke honestly about her feelings toward two church board members who opposed my leadership. Although she didn't name the individuals, she did express her feelings of anger, distrust, and dislike.

As the conflict escalated, some of her friends in the group eventually sided with those who were in conflict with me. It didn't take long for it to be reported at a congregational meeting that "it's no surprise that the pastor is at odds with the board; even his wife harbors bitterness in her heart against two board members." The speaker went on to quote what "she told me personally."

When honest feelings are used against us, there is no greater sense of betrayal.

When we came to our current church, Suzanne acknowledged to me that it would be harder for her to trust people in the new congregation because of the past. After hearing her honest admission, I began to notice that I, too, felt guarded in opening myself up to new friendships. Formerly we had given ourselves to people with great freedom; now both of us were more careful, more suspecting. Admitting that to each other drew us closer together.

Suzanne was in a "birthday club" with a group of women at a former church. She found it a wonderful source of friendship and support—until some of her birthday buddies turned against us. Not long ago I asked her if she would be interested in starting a birthday group at our current church. She didn't reply. She didn't have to. The look on her face told me everything I needed to know.

Trust betrayed is not easily rebuilt, and I learned again how I need to offer my wife support and space to allow her to heal—in her way and at her pace. There's no big secret about how I can make that happen. I simply need to listen and not be shocked at what she says or worried that she is not moving along fast enough in the healing process. Feelings of betrayal and distrust that go unacknowledged can drive us to bitterness and resentment. It's too easy to become cynical.

I used to be troubled by the wife of a friend who was formerly in the pastorate. Whenever Suzanne and I saw them, we knew we were in for an extended session of hearing about the foibles of their local fellowship. The woman would zing unnamed people in the congregation. She painted many in their congregation as hostile, carnal, set in their ways, and sinfully critical.

Rather than challenging her attitude, Suzanne and I tried to be as supportive and as caring as we could. Our listening slowly seemed to pay off. The couple realized we understood and genuinely cared for them. Finally, after one spate of sarcastic remarks, the wife blurted, "I guess by now you know how much I hate this church!"

We did know. It wasn't that we condoned her bitterness, but we understood it and were willing to put up with it until God pointed it out to her. I remember gently telling our friend, "Now that you've acknowledged that you hate them, I think you're ready to start forgiving them."

I've watched Suzanne struggle through disappointment and disillusionment with the church, and I've discovered the best thing I can do to help her is not to judge her attitude, to trust that God is at work in her, and to be emotionally present when she is ready to talk.

Family oasis

Recently Suzanne and I attended our denomination's retreat for pastoral couples in our region. We look forward to this conference every year. Out of this annual event, I struck up a friendship with a couple who caught my attention when I heard them speak about pastoring a church in the middle of a neighborhood in transition. The largely Anglo congregation was aging and resistant to change. Not only did the people in the church resist assimilating residents of their changing community, they wondered whether their pastor should remain in the church. Most wanted the good old days back. A once-thriving church was now torn by deep conflict, and the pastor was right in the middle of it, through no fault of his own.

As this couple told their story, I could sense their brokenness. The pastor's wife said, "If I didn't have my family with me through this past year, I would never have made it."

She then described how the love and support from their three sons had been their oasis. She told how the boys, who were in their twenties and all still lived in the area, dropped in for Sunday dinner after church. Along with the roast beef, potatoes and gravy, and apple pie, they shared laughter, pranks, teasing, and fun. It was as if for a few restful hours on a Sunday afternoon, she and her husband could forget the hassles at the church and be with the people who knew them best and loved them most. As she put it, "I never knew how much I would come to love, appreciate, and need my family." She added, "I knew the boys could have been doing lots of other things with their time on Sundays, but they chose to spend it with us—playing games, talking, and letting us know we were loved."

The hardest part was when late on Sundays this couple would say good-bye to their boys. It was made a little easier by their practice of standing in the living room, holding hands with their sons, and hearing each one pray for them. This couple said that at first it was difficult to tell their church struggles to their children. But they did, trying not to slander the people in the church, and the boys responded with support, which the parents had not expected.

There's nothing quite like the support of family during times of ministry crisis. Of course, our children can't be our therapists, and we need to sort judiciously through the information we tell them. But family members mean the most to us, and it is reassuring when they rally together for support and acceptance.

During the time when I was forced out of a pastorate (the story I tell in chapter 1), our family was a tremendous support. Although our boys were younger at the time, Suzanne and I tried to share with them our struggles at a level suitable to their understanding. They weren't old enough to grasp the details of the conflict, but they knew that it was time for our family to come together in support of one another.

It's a humbling experience to allow children to care for us during times of emotional crisis. We still recall with gratitude the evenings spent playing board games or putting together a jigsaw puzzle. Family hikes in the foothills, long mountain-bike treks, and canoe trips provided renewal and refreshment.

Shelter of friends

I have a theory that the longer a couple is in the pastorate, the smaller their circle of close friends becomes. In fact, if a couple isn't careful, the circle can become so small they may find that, after a while, they're the only ones in it.

Part of this stems from the distrust mentioned earlier. Yet we still need people in our lives who support and understand us. Close friends care for our souls when they are bruised.

I remember a friendship my wife developed shortly after one of our ministry miseries. In our conversations, Suzanne often quoted something her friend had said to her that provided comfort and empathy. Today she still keeps in contact with this friend whom God used in her life to embolden her faith and confidence in God's care.

One way we can help our wives weather church conflict is to encourage them to be open to a few trusted friends—outside of the immediate church situation or maybe just outside of the church, period. When I asked one pastor's wife how she coped with the conflict in a past church, she told me, "I didn't cope. It was only with the help of two loving Christian friends in my neighborhood that I even survived!"

Finding such a friend is not always easy. It takes patience and courage. One way to go about it is to ask God to show your wife someone who could be a safe friend. The woman who found friends in her neighborhood said that the person who became her special friend was someone she had only known as a casual acquaintance. She said, "One night I was praying and crying at the same time, asking God what I should do. Without thinking about it, suddenly Shannon's name popped into my head, and I knew right then that I needed to call her up and see if we could have coffee together." They did, and out of that came a friendship that provided much-needed support.

To this day, my wife talks about her friend Marcia

as one of the special people God used to help her through a difficult church experience. Marcia's favorite comment to her was that "It's okay to be who you are, because God has made you to be uniquely you."

In addition to friends and family, wives need their husbands during conflict. That sounds obvious, but I'm ashamed that I didn't realize how alone Suzanne felt. When she first told me that she felt alone, I asked, "You mean, alone other than for me?"

"No," Suzanne said. "I even feel separated from you."

Then she said, "Doesn't it matter to you that I feel like no one cares how I'm feeling, not even you?" She felt abandoned. I felt rebuked.

Since then I've tried to learn how to listen to her, be close to her, and draw her out to express what's going on inside. Although conflict isn't something to relish, I can say that some of the times when Suzanne and I felt the closest have been when we've walked through the fire together. We are learning to minister to each other.

When in the throes of a church conflict, our feelings are mirrored and usually intensified in our wives. A pastor can usually engage in the battle directly—he has to go to work and face the problem every day—thereby releasing some of his negative feelings, but his wife doesn't have that outlet. It's critical, therefore, that she find safe places to release her feelings, places where she is affirmed and where she can discover God's healing. The most obvious place where that needs to happen is at home with her husband.

7

STAYING BALANCED

IT HAD BEEN MONTHS SINCE I felt so refreshed. The time spent with my wife and two teenage sons during the summer had been some of the best in recent memory: a week at a ranch in the mountains, a family reunion at the "YMCA of the Rockies," camping, canoeing, and cookouts—all added up to a summer filled with memories and much needed renewal.

As the summer ended, I anticipated our next church board meeting, when our church leaders could renew our fellowship and refocus for the fall. Our meeting began as refreshing as I had anticipated. However, I noticed an unusual item on the agenda: member concerns. After our fellowship, prayer time, review of the minutes, and a financial update, the board chairman introduced a member who had some concerns.

In the following minutes, this person complained about the amount of summer vacation the board had approved for me. This member said, "We need our pastor to be here during summer weekends because new people visiting the church want to hear the pastor, not some second stringer they'll never see again."

After our guest left, the board discussed his concerns. That led to a discussion about what it means to lead a balanced life. Most board members admitted they would hardly be guilty of that. As I told of my commitment to a well-balanced life, the board seemed to see the complaint in a different light. Someone remarked, "I guess it's no surprise that we would have some complaints about the pastor's schedule. When you try to live a balanced life, there will probably be those who will think you aren't working hard enough."

Most church people don't share a uniform picture of what a balanced life looks like. I found that thinking specifically about my view of a healthy lifestyle is important if I am to give leadership in that area. But it's an area fraught with potential for conflict. No one will dispute that a pastor should live a balanced life, but when you live it out, you may hear rumblings. The truth is that if you develop other areas of your life outside of ministry, when extended church conflict sucks out the joy of ministry, you aren't cut down or completely devastated.

Philosophy of living

In general terms, I define a balanced life as a life lived according to biblical priorities. That seems simple enough. Most of what I've read or heard about priorities orders them numerically, from most important to least important. However, I have found the analogy of a pie more helpful to conceiving my philosophy than a numerical list, which implies I must fulfill my first priority before I can move on to the second. I see my priorities as pieces of a pie. Each piece is important (or else they would not be priorities!); the challenge is not to keep them in order but in balance.

For example, rather than striving to fulfill the priority of God in my life so I can get on to the priority of my wife, family, ministry, and, finally, community, I devote myself to all at the same time. Attempting to maintain equilibrium allows me to adjust the degree of focus I give my priorities at various times.

When I communicated this to the board, I used the discussion of my summer schedule to illustrate. I knew no one on the board doubted that pastoral ministry was a priority for me. I said, "I have an equal commitment to my wife and children and to my personal well-being, as well as to my relationship with God, and with my neighbors. The summer was an opportunity to focus more intently on my priorities of my wife and children rather than on the priority of church ministry."

One board member joked, "I guess the best way to discern whether your life is in balance is by the number of people who complain that you're not at the church enough!"

There may be more truth to that statement than most are willing to admit. Pastors often hold to an unwritten law that says we have to put in enough hours so that no one will ever doubt our commitment to sacrificial ministry. The last thing most of us want to hear is "I don't think you're working hard enough, Pastor."

I recently read an interview Jerry Falwell gave to *Christianity Today*, in which he stated he didn't think most pastors worked hard enough. That's a tough criticism. Most of us pride ourselves in being hard-working and diligent. Whenever someone questions my work ethic, my instinctive response is "I guess I'll just have to show you by putting in more hours."

Now I suggest another response to "Our pastor isn't putting in enough hours at the church": Ask that person, "Would you mind defining 'enough' for me?" Seldom have I heard an acceptable definition. Usually it is loosely defined as "at least as many hours as I put in at my job."

But I contend most professionals today put in too many hours at work.

How much is "enough"?

In formulating the specifics of a balanced life, I developed two criteria for the hours I spend at church:

1. *Are my working hours compatible with my current family situation?* Eighteen years ago, when I began my first pastorate, I asked my wife to help me be accountable for living a balanced life. She has exercised that right many times. Usually it comes as "The boys sure

miss you when you're gone this much." Or, "I miss taking our morning walks together." That is my cue that I need to rein in the priority of work so other priorities can regain equilibrium.

When our two boys were preschoolers, I spent fewer hours at the church than I do now that they are teenagers. I arrived at the office earlier in the morning to compensate for an early departure; I was almost always home by 4:30 in the afternoon. By then my wife needed a break from the kids, so I arranged to play with the boys while she took some time for herself. She not only appreciated the break, she also has expressed numerous times how much she appreciated the fact that I was sensitive to her needs and put them on equal par with ministry.

2. *Does my work schedule set a positive example?* Or does it reinforce the imbalanced work priority of the men and women in the church?

If I regularly work seven days a week and put in 60, 70, or 80 hours a week, how can I challenge someone who is doing the same to the detriment of his or her family? I have had numerous conversations with a man in my congregation about his work habits; he works at least 70 hours a week. His wife has talked to my wife about how to handle his work schedule, which is putting pressure on their marriage and family.

Last week he told me, "If you can find some balance in life with all the demands on you as pastor of this church, then with God's help so can I. I'm making plans to back off at work after the first of the year." He has hired a new assistant to cover some of his responsibilities and is training two other people to assist him with other phases of his job. He even asked me if I would hold him accountable.

I can hear the objection of some: "But what about getting your work done? How can you possibly get enough accomplished if you spend only 50 to 55 hours a week in ministry?"

My response is simple: "Would you mind defining 'enough' for me?"

While I know my work is never done, I've discovered I need the discipline to say, "I'm finished." Knowing when to finish each workday is crucial to a balanced life.

Schooling the church

As a pastor I work more like a traveling salesman or consultant than an engineer in an office. I'm working when I'm at my desk, of course, but I am also working when I visit a child in the hospital or eat lunch with a new couple in the church or spend the day in prayer at a mountain retreat or have folks over for dessert on a Sunday evening. I'm working even though my car may not be in the church parking lot. That's what I have to communicate to the church.

A pastor-friend came up with a creative way to remind people of this in the office-hours sign he posted on his door. It reads:

Office Hours:

> I'm here most days about 8 or 9 A.M. Occasionally I arrive as early as 7 A.M., but some days I get here as late as 10 or 11 A.M. I usually leave about 4 or 5 P.M., but occasionally I'm out of here around 6 or 8 P.M. Sometimes I leave as late as 11 P.M. Some days or afternoons or mornings I'm not here at all, and lately I've been here just about all the time, except when I'm someplace else, but I should be here then, too.

I want to help our church recognize that I work differently than most professionals. That is an ongoing challenge, and the way pastors work will never be fully understood by everyone. I have had countless discussions with boards, staff, and church members about living a balanced life. Only once was I chastised for attempting to keep work in balance with the rest of life's priorities. All the other times people have appreciated my openness and honesty.

The good from these discussions about my work ethic has been enormous. Regularly I print a summary of my work schedule in our church bulletin or newsletter so people will know when I am available to meet with them for routine issues. (Emergencies, of course, don't need to fit the schedule.)

My secretary submits a simple announcement for the bulletin that runs once a month. It reads:

For your convenience in meeting with the pastor, his schedule is as follows (please call the church office to schedule an appointment as his "office" hours are not always spent "in" the office):

Monday: Office in morning; staff meeting 11:30 A.M. to 2 P.M.; office in afternoon

Tuesday: Office all day

Wednesday: Study/prayer day

Thursday: Sermon work in morning; office in afternoon

Friday: Day off (please call the church office with any emergencies)

Saturday & Sunday: Available by appointment; Sat. evening reserved for Sunday preparations

Weekday evenings: Available by appointment, though limited to three evenings for meetings or appointments.

I want people to know my work schedule is their business, too, and I gladly share it with them. I give them the right to address my priorities, but I also tell them that assumes I have the same right with them.

I discuss my schedule with the church board at least twice a year. I do this at the beginning of the fall and then again at the onset of summer. I want the board to know that my schedule changes the most at these two times of the year. I solicit their input and questions about the schedule. That also provides the board an opportunity to discuss their priorities and lifestyle.

Exception to the rule

Some pastors, of course, might be tempted to work too little, but in my experience and conversations with them, that is the exception.

One time, however, some in our church began to question the work ethic of a staff pastor. I took their concerns seriously, just as I would if a person were spending too much time at the church. Rather than camouflage my inquiry about his work schedule, I told the staff member straight out that some folks felt he might not be working enough hours. That enabled us to deal with the issue head on.

I asked the staff person about his usual work hours. After calculating his hours, I said that to me they seemed a little light. I usually require staff to work between 42 and 45 hours per week. He explained his concern about being home for his wife and their three young children. That was legitimate. I explored with him alternate work hours that would not place such a burden on his family. We finally arrived at a plan that was balanced yet provided for five more hours of work each week.

The next step was to communicate that plan to those concerned as well as to the segment of the church he ministered to directly. I addressed those who raised the issue by writing them a letter saying that the stage of this pastor's family required that he spend more time at home. I then detailed how he would compensate for that by revising his schedule to work at other times. I thanked them for their concern, assuring them I would monitor his schedule for the near future.

The staff pastor then printed his schedule in the next newsletter and posted it on his office door. For the next month, he provided me with a weekly review of how he was managing his schedule.

Strong in all events

Such upfront communication has affected the church's attitude toward my work and my need for balance. At a recent newcomers social, I overheard a board member telling a newcomer, "We try to protect the pastor's time and schedule so he can do what he needs to do in the church and also have time for the other priorities in his life."

I couldn't have said it any better.

There will always be those who question my definition of balance or the way I work it out week to week. There have been times when I put in 40 hours and called it quits because of other priorities.

Have I ever regretted it? Occasionally. But then I see how my attempt to be balanced affects my relationship with God, my wife, children, church, and friends. In the final analysis, I want to be a person and pastor who can say, "I have finished the race in all the events where God had me entered."

8

ANGELS IN THE ROIL

I REMEMBER THE FIRST ANGEL I MET. It happened at the outset of our honeymoon as my wife and I traveled down the Amalfi coast in southern Italy. Suddenly the Fiat van we were driving stopped running. No amount of tinkering or praying would restart it.

We knew we had stopped along a dangerous stretch of road on a twisted drive that wound along the beautiful coast just south of Naples. This section of the Amalfi Drive was infamous for its bandits and thieves. If there was a road in southern Italy comparable to the road between Jerusalem and Jericho, this was it. Suzanne and I were mindful of what Jesus said happened to the man on that road.

After the Fiat wheezed its last breath, we set off to find the nearest town, several kilometers away. The area was too dangerous for one of us to stay with the car, so we gathered as many of our belongings as we could carry and put our thumbs in the air to hitch a ride. We were certain this would be the last we would see of our car and the belongings left in it. We wanted only to make it safely to the next town.

As we huddled close to the cobblestone wall separating the narrow road from the cliff dropping precipitously to the sea, we prayed that God would put angels around the car to protect it while we were gone and also send an angel to deliver us safely to the nearest town. Just then a car came screeching around the curve behind our disabled vehicle. The driver saw our thumbs in the air and immediately hit the brakes and wheeled his Alfa Romeo up close to the rock wall. We weren't sure whether we should run or risk talking to this man. Before we could decide, the Italian driver was out of his car and asked us with a disarming smile, *You need a ride to Ravello, don't you?*

We nodded, and the next thing we knew we were on our way.

Our rescuer turned out to be wonderfully kind and gracious. He dropped us off at our hotel and drove away with a warm *Ciao, arrivederci!* The next words out of my wife's mouth were, "I think we just rode with an angel."

I was sure of it.

The next morning we were in no hurry to return to where we had left our van the night before. Figuring it would be vandalized or stolen, we alerted the police before a missionary friend picked us up at the hotel to take us back to assess the damage. As we rounded the last turn, we saw our Fiat parked next to the stone wall. Quickly surveying its condition, we discovered in our hasty departure we had left the rear door unlocked. As we peered inside to see if anything was left, we were shocked to see that nothing had been disturbed. Not even the rear door had been opened. Everything was exactly as we had left it!

Had God indeed given his angels charge over that van to protect it from thieves? It certainly seemed so.

I've thought about our "Amalfi angels" often during times of turmoil in ministry. When I've felt buffeted by those storms, I've found myself again asking God to send his angels of protection and comfort.

Does he respond? Yes, always. Maybe not in the way I would have envisioned or petitioned, but God does care and he does act. We have his Word on it (1 Pet. 5:7). God does not pick and choose which circumstances he will use to execute his will in our lives. Rather, "in all things God works for the good of those who love him" (Rom. 8:28). The challenge is to learn how to recognize God at work and listen to his voice when we're distracted by the suffering of ministry.

Back when the telegraph was the fastest means of long-distance communication, there was a story, perhaps apocryphal, about a young man who applied for a job as a Morse code operator. Answering an ad in the newspaper, he went to the address that was listed. When he arrived, he entered a large, noisy office. In the background a telegraph clacked away. A sign on the receptionist's counter instructed job applicants to fill out a form and wait until they were summoned to enter the inner office.

The young man completed his form and sat down with seven other waiting applicants. After a few minutes, the young man stood up, crossed the room to the door of the inner office, and walked right in. Naturally the other applicants perked up, wondering what was going on. Why had this man been so bold? They muttered among themselves that they hadn't heard any summons yet. They took more than a little satisfaction in assuming the young man who went into the office would be reprimanded for his presumption and summarily disqualified for the job.

Within a few minutes the young man emerged from the inner office escorted by the interviewer, who announced to the other applicants, "Gentlemen, thank you very much for coming, but the job has been filled by this young man."

The other applicants began grumbling to one another. Then one spoke up, saying, "Wait a minute—I don't understand something. He was the last one to come in, and we never even got a chance to be interviewed. Yet he got the job. That's not fair."

The employer responded, "I'm sorry, but all the time you've been sitting here, the telegraph has been ticking out the following message in Morse code: 'If you understand this message, then come right in. The job is yours.' None of you heard it or understood it. This young man did. So the job is his."

God uses many means to demonstrate his care— not only through his Word, his Spirit, and the ministry of Christian friends, but also through more unconventional methods—like burning bushes, talking donkeys, hungry creatures of the sea, visiting angels, or a bright star in the darkened sky. We need only to be alert to these signs. That God cares for us during conflict is certain.

Word and Spirit

I am always amazed at the apostle Paul's sensitivity to God's work in his life. He could see the signs of God's work in the darkest of circumstances. As Paul's life was drawing to a close in the prison in Rome, he told Timothy that at one point it was only the Lord who stood at his side and gave him strength (2 Tim. 4:17). The believers had deserted him, and Paul was left alone to defend himself against his accusers—but he knew God was strengthening him.

Once I had lunch with a man who had allied himself with a group in the church that was in opposition to me and the staff. This man hadn't heard the whole story, yet he was sure who needed exhortation. As I listened, I could feel my anger rising and I wanted to set him straight. But before I could launch into my defense, I sensed the voice of the Spirit within me: "Let go of this. I will deal with these accusations." I reluctantly saved that piece of my mind for another day and left our lunch meeting saying only, "I will give some prayerful thought to what you've said."

Just before noon the next day, this man hurried into my office on his way to a meeting nearby and told me in a whispered tone, "I'm sorry for what I said to you yesterday. I discovered last night that I had listened to only one side of the story and then I jumped to false conclusions."

Had I not sensed God's work through the Holy Spirit the day before, I probably would have responded in anger to the accusations, fueling the fire.

Not only have I sensed the Holy Spirit's nudging during church conflict, I've also experienced God's care through the Word. Passages of Scripture I have read and studied a dozen times have on certain occasions unexpectedly spoken to my soul with new intimacy, power, and relevance. On the other hand, the Holy Spirit has also used sections of Scripture that I am largely unfamiliar with to extend his care for me.

After being terminated from our church, my wife and I attended a pastors' conference at Sonscape Ministries in Colorado. As I wrote earlier, that time was a wonderful week of renewal and healing for us. One highlight was the evening of worship and Communion. Throughout the day leading up to that evening, the Lord had drawn near to both Suzanne and me through his Word. That evening as we knelt together before the Communion table, we shared with each other the promises that God had given us from the Word during the day—our first opportunity that day to do that.

Earlier that afternoon I had marked in my Bible a powerful promise God had shown me in Isaiah 43. I was anxious to share it with Suzanne. But first I asked her what God had shown her that day. She opened her Bible and read:

> But now, this is what the Lord says.... Fear not, for I have redeemed you; I have summoned you by name; you are mine. When you pass through the waters, I will be with you; and when you pass through the rivers, they will not sweep over you. When you walk through the fire, you will not be burned; the flames will not set you ablaze. For I am the Lord, your God, the Holy One of Israel, your Savior.... Since you are precious and honored in my sight, and because I love you, I will give men in exchange for you, and people in exchange for your life. Do not be afraid, for I am with you.

I could not respond to her after she finished reading; I was overcome with emotion. Those were the exact promises from Isaiah 43:1–5 that God had given to me that afternoon to comfort me and encourage me to press ahead amid my doubts about staying in ministry.

I've discovered that even when I have not recognized his care immediately, it is still there like the net below a high-wire acrobat. During the course of his act, the acrobat is oblivious to the net below. As the act proceeds and the daring stunts are completed with perfection, the performer has no need to recognize the presence of the net. But when the artist falls, he owes his life to the net. I've learned to be more aware of God's net in my life, to try to see how God is caring for me during hard times. In episodes of conflict, I frequently will begin a day by praying, "Lord, help me to see you at work in and around me today."

What God often shows me is how he is working through the ministry of other believers in the body of Christ.

Friends like Timothy

The apostle Paul was certainly aware of the care of other believers. His letters are a record of his gratitude to others—Epaphroditus (Phil. 2:25), Timothy (Phil. 2:19ff), Tychicus (Col. 4:7), Aristarchus, Mark, Justus (Col. 4:10ff), and Luke (2 Tim. 4:11), to name just a few.

Sometimes those who have cared for me have been those I would have expected. Other times God has surprised me with someone unexpected, and I've wondered, *Where did that person come from?* The days after the phone call informing me of my termination from ministry were unbearably long. I can hardly remember the events of that first week, the shock of being cut off from my work, even my calling, was so great.

I can recall, though, one day in that week—Wednesday evening. As my wife and I sat in our living room that evening, the phone finally rang. It was a call from a friend who is a Christian counselor. Our families had been close friends when they lived in our city, but since they had moved back East two years before, we had kept in touch only through Christmas cards. Because of our infrequent contact, I knew he wasn't calling about the crisis at hand; he had no way of knowing. He was calling to say hello and to get the phone number of a mutual friend.

I asked my wife if she could find the phone number he wanted. We continued to chat, and he suddenly stopped mid-sentence and asked carefully, "By the way, are you guys okay? Maybe there's more reason for my call than getting that phone number."

"Funny you should ask," I said, "and even stranger that you would call tonight . . ."

For the next thirty minutes he listened, prayed, and spoke a few well-chosen words of love and encouragement. When we finally said good-bye, it felt like I had fallen straight into the net below me. The call was like receiving a direct message from God.

For a few minutes after I hung up the phone, Suzanne and I reflected on God's care through that friend. The phone rang again. It was the same friend.

"I really did call earlier just to get that phone number," he said. "Do you have it?"

In addition to care that has seemed like direct intervention by God, I've also been strengthened from a small band of friends who have walked with me through life over the years. The older I get the more thankful I am for such friends. The apostle Paul, too, had friends who rallied around him during hard times. When Paul was a lonely prisoner facing his final days in the Mamertine Prison in Rome, he asked for Timothy. That faithful friend had knit his heart with Paul's. They had been together from the early days of Paul's missionary ministry. As comrades they had navigated the waters of the Aegean Sea and traversed the countryside of Macedonia. It was to Timothy that Paul had entrusted his beloved flock of Ephesus. If anyone cared for Paul and would be there at the end, it was Timothy. He knew even the very coat that Paul missed and wanted to have returned—the one he had left at Carpus's home in Troas.

More important, Paul needed the scrolls and parchments. The documents were among his most treasured possessions. The coat was practical, but the parchments were essential. Those portions of Scripture would bring ultimate comfort to Paul as he read the psalms of David, the wisdom of Solomon, and the exhortations of the prophets. Timothy could be trusted to carry those treasures.

Finally, Paul confessed that he needed Timothy— not for what Timothy could bring him or do for him. He needed Timothy, his friend.

"Timothy, I need you to come and be with me. And do your best to get here before winter."

As far as we know, those were Paul's final written words, directed to a friend who was like no other.

God has sent to me Timothy-like friends, whose care has come in many forms—a note, a phone call, a financial gift, or simply the opportunity to withdraw in solitude to their vacation home. I've even sensed their care when they have looked me in the eye and told me where they thought I might be off track in what I had said or done.

Suzanne and I have talked about how rare in pastoral ministry those kinds of relationships are. Too often we are seen as set apart from ordinary believers in the church—not "ordinary" enough to befriend. I have tried to dispel that myth, but cultivating friendship in pastoral work requires a special commitment. I have made a conscious effort to spend time with Christian men inside and outside the church with whom I have sensed a connection. When I find someone I think I can reveal my heart to, it's as if I have discovered gold.

In the past year, our church has been experiencing a bit of God's pruning. From the custodian to my closest associate pastor, every staff member has moved on. The reasons have seemed legitimate: marriage, spouse job relocation, graduate school, physical impairment, and a different ministry calling. But the effect on the church has been huge. People are feeling uncertain, disconnected, dispirited, and a bit fearful about the future. I share much of their emotional and spiritual malaise.

Shortly after the resignations began, a friend in the church asked me after the Sunday worship service, "Can I come by this week and pray with you?" He came by on Tuesday morning, and our time together stretched well into the afternoon; we talked and prayed intermittently for several hours. When he left he said, "I'd like to do this with you again next week, if you have the time." The next Tuesday we prayed together a second time.

Over the ensuing weeks, that person became my confidant. He has been relentless in his care and in gathering other men around me to pray for me and to voice their support and encouragement. Not a week goes by that he doesn't send a note or make a phone call to me in addition to our regular prayer times. His family has taken a special interest in our family; we have become a part of their morning prayer circle as they ask God to protect and bless us.

They are God's net, spread beneath us during this time of testing and trial. Had I not learned to recognize how God cares for us during previous difficult times, I would see them only as concerned friends. Or I might be a bit more cynical and view them suspiciously, wondering if they have a hidden agenda. But now I see them as agents of God himself.

By taking the risk of letting others care for us, we can reap lasting rewards. In addition to the obvious benefit of a true friendship is the joy of experiencing in their care the work of God. Angels come in many guises.

9

WHEN TO BACK OFF

OUR FAMILY IS LEARNING A LOT about lacrosse these days. It's a relatively new sport in our part of the country, but our younger son plays it. We're learning the various techniques for handling the ball, attacking the opponent, scoring goals, and defending one's net.

In a recent game as I watched our son play his position, I was confused by the movements he was making on the field. After the game I asked, "What were those moves you were making out there when your opponent was guarding you?" He replied, somewhat sheepishly, "Oh, I was just trying to avoid letting that big guy crush me!"

I laughed with him: "It's always a good idea to know how to keep from getting crushed!"

I have had to learn a similar strategy in ministry: There are times when the best way to deal with conflict is to avoid it in the first place.

When I was a boy trying to get along with kids in the schoolyard, my father used to tell me, "The easiest fights to win are the ones you stay out of." He was right, of course. But that's easier said than done. I have a cartoon on the side of my filing cabinet that shows the pastor behind the pulpit on Sunday morning saying, "I interrupt this sermon to inform you that the fourth-grade boys are now in complete control of their Sunday school class. And they are holding Miss Mosby hostage at this very moment." That's a light way of talking about a painful truth: church conflicts can be nasty and bruising affairs, hazardous to the health of both the pastor and the church.

How do we stay out of a hostage situation? It's not something discussed in seminary, or if it was, I was gone that day. I've learned the hard way, through years of mistakes caused by a brash style of leadership that alienated those who did not share my take-no-prisoners approach. I thought I was doing the work of God with passion and zeal. I accepted nothing less than total commitment from myself—the problem was I had the same rigid expectations of others. I believed that conflict was the natural companion of devoted service to Christ.

In time and in pain, I learned otherwise. God showed me that to avoid conflict is not to be lukewarm or unspiritual; on the contrary, Scripture pronounces a specific blessing on those who excel in the art of peacemaking. Jesus said, "Blessed are the peacemakers, for they will be called sons of God" (Matt. 5:9). I have learned to extend more grace to others and build more lasting relationships through mutual ministry. I now know that while no pastorate will be conflict-free, neither should conflict be shrugged off as an occupational hazard a pastor has to live with.

Effective ministry does not have to be carried out in a hostile environment.

Battle choosing

It was a great revelation to me to discover that not every battle is worth waging and not all conflict is worthy of my engagement. Some incendiary issues simply need to be avoided. When Nehemiah was leading the rebuilding of the wall of Jerusalem, he had plenty of opportunities for conflict. I am continually amazed at his skill in deciding which conflicts were worthy of his response and which were to be ignored so the work could continue.

After repeated attempts from Sanballat, Tobiah, and Geshem to thwart Nehemiah's efforts, they concocted a scheme to get rid of him once and for all (Neh. 6). Their ploy was to lure him to the peace table so they could ambush him. Rather than confronting this trio of trouble head on, Nehemiah sidestepped their trap. He simply sent his regrets: "I am carrying on a great project and cannot go down. Why should the work stop while I leave it and go down to you?" (Neh. 6:4).

While writing this chapter, I had an opportunity to practice some of what I'd learned from Nehemiah. Normally I receive from our worship team the service plan two weeks in advance. However, due to spring break for our school district, a number of the team leaders were out of town, and so I didn't get the worship service plan until the Monday before. There were a couple of significant problems with the service that I felt would adversely affect the flow of worship. I called our lay worship leader and talked to him about the changes I thought were necessary to allow for a better worship flow and build a stronger worship experience.

Somewhat reluctantly, he agreed to make the changes.

Then on Saturday evening I received an e-mail from him informing me that he had reconsidered, and he now wanted to stick to the original service plan. He said he was "sure I'd understand."

There was a time in my ministry when I would have been on the phone two minutes later, demanding an explanation. In a diplomatic but direct way, I would have reminded him that the proper way to handle something like this is through personal conversation, not by e-mail, and that since I was the one ultimately responsible for the worship services, we would do it the way I proposed.

This time I took a deep breath, prayed that God would bless the service, and asked him to help me be gracious and affirming toward our worship leader and the worship team on Sunday morning. I then put the matter to rest for the remainder of the evening. On Sunday morning I acknowledged to our worship leader that I had received his e-mail, thanked him for thinking the situation through, and affirmed his decision to proceed with the service as originally planned. Nothing more was said about any changes to the service.

That response settled the issue.

The service proceeded as planned. While, in my humble opinion, the flow felt slightly disjointed during the early part of the worship, no one seemed to notice. Afterward I thanked God for his wisdom in teaching me how to choose my battles carefully.

When to go to the mat

In deciding which issues are significant enough to confront and run the risk of conflict, I usually ask myself three questions:

1. *Does the situation involve something that is contrary to our mission as a church?* If the issue before me does not conflict with our church's mission of helping people discover a personal relationship with God and become fully devoted followers of Jesus Christ, then I begin to think of it as something that ought to be left alone or dealt with in a nonconfrontational manner.

The leader of our worship team does a fine job leading worship, but he struggles to communicate with the worship team and staff. One team member recently told me, "We would work well together if we just didn't have to communicate."

It is not that the worship leader does not communicate; it is the *way* he communicates. He prefers not to speak face-to-face with people; he uses faxes, voice mail, e-mail, or memos. Seldom does he speak face-to-face with someone for more than thirty seconds.

Rather than making his style of communication into a huge issue, I've told people to be willing to adapt to his methods. In addition, I've suggested to the team to take the initiative in setting up meetings with him, with every member of the team present. As the leader has heard from the team how much they appreciate personal interaction with him, he is becoming more receptive to adapting his style of communication.

2. *Does the issue cause us to compromise our commitment to being and building faithful followers of Christ?* A problem arose with our adult-class leadership teams, which were not adequately preparing for their Sunday morning classes. This was hindering our efforts to model and teach the principle that we offer our best to God in serving him, so I decided that we needed to address the issue directly with the class leaders. I attended the monthly leadership team meeting for one of the classes and asked if I could speak to them about the issue. I explained, "This issue is not just about what day of the week you prepare your lesson or the amount of time it takes you to prepare for it. It is about us in leadership providing a model for the church body about the cost of serving Christ.

"If we are willing to pay that price in the small things, then God can entrust us with much larger responsibilities and give greater blessing to our service."

There was nothing but graciousness in the reply of the leaders. They committed to strengthen that area. One leader replied lightheartedly, "If you call me on any Saturday this month and my lesson is not already 80 percent prepared, then I promise I'll eat the coffee grounds in front of the class on Sunday morning!"

3. *In one year will it make a difference in our church whether we dealt with this issue?* If it seems to me that the situation is not going to make a difference in the church that anyone will remember or recognize in a year, then I am inclined to leave it alone or at least not deal with it in a confrontational way.

It's amazing how few issues will be significant or even remembered in a year. What makes many of them significant or remembered is not the issues themselves but the degree of conflict they needlessly caused. I try to evaluate the "one-year significance" of potentially volatile issues and use that as an indicator of whether a situation should be avoided or addressed.

One challenge in our congregation is to get people in our Christian education ministries to arrive early enough to set up their classes by the time class is supposed to start. I'm often told that "for years our church has been 'flexible' with the time the Sunday morning Bible Discovery Hour begins." In essence, that means a couple classes start at 9:15 A.M., the scheduled start time, but others begin at 9:30 or even 9:45.

No one got too worked up about that—except me!

I was tempted to attend the Christian education leadership meeting and announce that we would no longer have a delayed start on Sunday mornings. But then I asked myself, *Is having all the classes start on time really going to make a significant difference in the church next year?*

Since the education ministry was growing and had not been starting on time for years before I arrived, I had to answer no. I left the issue alone and labeled it "one of the quirks of our church." There was no confrontation and thus no conflict.

If I answer no to all three questions, that tells me the issue is not worth risking conflict.

Integrity slide

A family in our church recently had their basement finished by a contractor. The process ended up being one of those construction nightmare stories. I knew both parties in the debacle and somehow got myself in the middle of the dispute.

As the conflict became more ugly, I received calls from both sides; each party tried to use me to reinforce their case. Such conversations turned negative quickly. The homeowner once told me, "And not only does he [the contractor] do shoddy work, but I've heard stories about how unethical he has been in paying former employees."

The contractor was guilty of the same low blows as the conflict escalated.

Eventually, I found myself succumbing to the temptation of letting my knowledge of the other party leak out in conversations with each side. It wasn't until too late that I caught myself and moved back to a neutral position. But by then I had already said too much. One party confronted me about my loose tongue. I had to admit my error and then I went back to the other party and did the same. In the end, my error turned out to be a lesson for all three of us; the two parties admitted they had made the same mistake.

Conflict has a way of growing from a small snowslide into a full-scale avalanche, and on its way downhill it can sweep victims into its wake. A conflict has the potential to mar the integrity of combatants on both sides. That happens as each side seeks to garner support for its position—making exaggerated statements, shading the truth, impugning the motives of others.

How can we guard against this? One important step is to refuse to discuss the relevant issues with anyone other than those directly involved. We need to be truthful in citing the facts of a situation and not exaggerate the details. When we maintain our integrity, not only are we exhibiting Christlike behavior, but also we don't risk losing our credibility with others—including those who may be on the other side of the argument.

A good friend of mine recently resigned from his church after more than a year of unrelenting conflict. The vast majority of people in the church were shocked to hear of his resignation. Most had no idea there was even a problem brewing in the church.

I asked him how that could be when the conflict was so severe. His response spoke volumes about his integrity throughout the ordeal. He said, "I never spoke about the problems with anyone in the church who was not directly involved. And those on the other side of the issue only spoke to each other with whom they were in agreement."

Just because our adversaries may use a certain battle plan does not justify our following suit if it calls us to compromise our integrity. As Oswald Chambers once wrote, "To see that my adversary gives me my rights is natural; but from our Lord's standpoint it does not matter if I am defrauded or not; what does matter is that I do not defraud."

My friend's response to the conflict in his church was a powerful example of what I call incarnational leadership. It's the kind of leadership that Jesus would exhibit in the church—a leadership that refuses to win the battle at *any* cost. The victory won at the expense of our integrity is no victory at all.

Ounce of prevention

The sparse instruction I received in seminary on dealing with people and issues in the church could be put on a single piece of paper. However, there was one bit of counsel that was given among those limited lessons that could have saved me volumes of anguished journal entries. A pastor who was an adjunct professor said, "Work harder at maintaining relationships in the church than you do at solving problems in the church."

His point was that if we focus on building and maintaining healthy, redemptive relationships with people, we will have far fewer problems to solve—and fewer problems means less conflict.

It was a wise statement, one that I wish I would have heeded more often in my early years of ministry. I wish I'd asked myself two questions: (1) Is this battle worth the cost of a broken relationship? (2) Is there another way of dealing with the conflict that won't damage relationships?

A leader in one church I served was forever confronting me with ways in which I didn't measure up to his expectations. It seemed my suggestions were seldom accepted, and my best efforts were usually not good enough. The strain on our relationship was so great that we seldom spoke to each other. We didn't have a heated argument; we simply shut the other out.

After months of cold war, one Sunday he confronted me about a worship issue. I had felt convicted that our relationship wasn't what it should be and was praying that God would provide a way for us to reconcile.

Several minutes after the confrontation, I walked back to where this man was standing and asked if we could talk. I told him I didn't want the conflict between us to continue. I sincerely apologized to him for my wrong attitude and actions, and asked for his forgiveness. He granted it immediately and then threw his arms around me. In my ear, he whispered, "I've so needed to hear you say that, more than you'll ever know. I only hope I can do the same one of these days."

I knew what he meant. People who knew him were aware he seldom if ever admitted he was wrong about something. I didn't expect I would hear an apology from him, but at least I had taken care of my shortcomings.

To make sure he knew I wanted a fresh start, I invited him to be my prayer partner two weeks later. I pray with someone from the church every Tuesday, and on his first Tuesday to pray, he arrived a little early. We talked a bit and then moved to my office to pray. Just before we finished praying, he stopped and said, "I want you to know that I am sorry for the way I treated you the past year. It was wrong, and I need your forgiveness just like you asked for mine."

That confession melted away the last bit of hurt from the protracted conflict with him. Again, we embraced, and both of us acknowledged our new friendship was more important than any issue we had or would face. Since then we have built on that commitment to the point that we are becoming good friends.

In my recreational reading, I enjoy books on the history of various wars the United States has waged. I've learned a lot from studying Abraham Lincoln's leadership during the Civil War. Near the end of the war, when the scalawags were busy lording it over their Southern countrymen, a hot-blooded contingency of diehard Confederate rebels gained an audience with the president to address the issue. Lincoln's gentle, friendly manner with the group soon thawed the ice and the Southerners left with a new respect for their old foe. A Northern congressman approached the president and criticized him for befriending the enemy. Instead, he said, Lincoln should have had them shot for the traitors they were. Lincoln smiled and replied, "Am I not destroying my enemies by making them my friends?"

10

OUT OF THE PAIN

I HAD JUST GOTTEN OFF the phone with a man on the church board. He had called to warn me that my leading antagonist, also a member of the board, was going to confront me that evening at the board meeting. He was going to recommend the board reverse its previous decisions affirming the direction and mission of the church.

Without warning, my blood pressure went through the roof and I yelled, "I don't believe this is happening. This means war!" My secretary came running into my office and asked what was going on. I told her, "We're about to have the battle of this church's life at tonight's board meeting."

Over the next few minutes, I turned into an infantry commander as I stormed through the office barking out orders to the staff. I wanted to gather damaging information about this board member, and I knew exactly where he was most vulnerable—his giving record. I asked the financial secretary to give me a printout of the man's contributions over the past two years. The report reinforced my suspicions: this wealthy individual had given only $300 to the church during that time. I planned to take that report to the meeting, throw it on the table at the appropriate time, and say, "Gentlemen, do we want to hear more criticism and vitriol from someone who has invested so little in our church?"

If that didn't put him in his place, nothing would.

Fortunately, I didn't carry through with my plan, even though it seemed like the right tactic to silence my opposition for good. Now I'm a little embarrassed about it.

One of my favorite features in magazines and newspapers is the "Where Are They Now?" type of segment that focuses on the lives of well-known people from a then-and-now perspective. It's interesting to discover the direction someone's life has taken since he or she was in the public eye. I find value in that kind of reflection in my own life as well, especially as it relates to events that were significant in some way. Writing this book gave me a then-and-now look at my life since I left the church I described in the opening chapter. I can now see from this side of the conflict that God used my experience to deepen me—as a pastor and as a person.

Most of the lessons I've learned are woven into the previous pages of this book, but as I reflect on years of journal writing, I realize that through ministry conflict, God has helped me discover what kind of good he brings out of pain.

Hurt that refines

When I was in seminary I heard a speaker make a statement that at the time I scarcely believed. Quoting A. W. Tozer, the speaker said, "God cannot use a man greatly until he has hurt him deeply." Around the same time I read a similar observation by Alan Redpath: "When God wants to do an impossible task, he takes an impossible person and crushes him."

Could that possibly be true? I wondered. *Does God ever bring hurt to our lives—even for the purpose of refining us or increasing our usefulness?*

Many years and many hurts later, I've come to learn that there are lessons in life that can only be learned through God's curriculum of pain. That's part of what Jesus was getting at in John 15:2 when he told his disciples that "every branch that does bear fruit he prunes so that it will be even more fruitful."

For example, pain has taught me to be more empathetic with people who are in need. At a pastor/spouse retreat, I remember hearing a friend tell of the difficulties he had experienced in his church that past year. He talked of misunderstandings, hurt feelings, and harsh accusations that had erupted in the church. Several key leadership families had left, and he and his wife were feeling whipped and beaten.

I wasn't prepared for the rush of emotion that came over me. Suddenly I could *feel* the pain he felt as though it were my own. I had felt that pain only a year and a half earlier. When he finished, I embraced him and his wife. Several others joined the circle, and our prayers for them issued from hearts knit together by our mutual experiences of pain.

Another way God has used pain in my life is to make me more relaxed and patient with people. My ideas and desires for the church are no longer so important that they have to be accepted right away, if at all. I acknowledge now that God may use someone else's idea to accomplish his work in our church. I've also learned to concede the fact that people don't always perform as I'd like. I realize that healthy relationships are more important than merely getting the job done. Even as I write this, these lessons seem so obvious, so basic to pastoral work. But they were murder to learn.

Not long ago I was working with our elder board to hire a new staff member. I felt the process was not moving along as quickly as I thought it should. A couple of elders had not completed their assigned tasks as scheduled, and because of this we couldn't make any final decisions. A few years ago I might have gotten angry or impatient. Now I said, "What's more important than getting this new position finalized is what's going on in your lives. Obviously there are some things happening there that God is using to revise our schedule for this decision. Let's relax and follow God's lead in this issue."

I wasn't excusing someone's inattention or irresponsibility. I had, however, learned to be more sensitive to someone else's *life*—the struggles that may have affected his work.

All in the waiting

I remember my first roller coaster ride as a kid. It happened at a later age for me than it did for most of my friends. Even my younger brother had ridden a roller coaster before I had. But I was cautious, even fearful. Finally, with the urging of my older brother and my father—and feeling embarrassed that my younger brother had taken the plunge first—I screwed up enough courage and allowed my dad to take me on the coaster.

My father kept assuring me that everything would be okay. His last words were, "If it gets too scary, just tuck your head under my arm, and I'll hang on to you." From the moment the roller coaster crested the first hill until we rolled to a stop, my head was buried in his armpit. I knew that my dad would never intentionally try to hurt me or put me at risk. If he said I'd be safe, I'd be safe. That didn't take the fear out of the ride for me, but it did allow me to stay close to him during the ride. In a similar way, the pain of being forced out of a church led me to trust God in a way that I had never done before. Although I had no understanding of what God was doing or why, I discovered that he could be trusted completely to bring me through the ordeal. I believed and would discover again that God had not been caught off guard. He wasn't wringing his hands and wondering, *What am I going to do with Preston now?* Pain was part of God's curriculum for my life, and I needed to learn to trust him through it.

I don't know what prompted me to trust God. The trust was just there. Perhaps it was the deposit of years of Bible study, preaching, and teaching. What I knew in my head was now being called into service. During the first few days after my resignation, I recalled God's curriculum for Moses' life. According to Exodus 2, Moses ended up at the well in Midian, where he sat down, probably with his face buried in his hands, feeling like a failure. He would remain in the desert of Midian for the next forty years, tending the flock of sheep owned by his father-in-law, Jethro. Moses was there because he had killed the Egyptian. But rather than blaming God or carping at him for not preventing his situation, Moses waited and hoped and trusted. Moses trusted that somehow God was still in control and hoped that someday he would again call Moses to serve him.

That trust was well placed, for eventually God remembered his covenant with his people and went looking for Moses on the far side of the desert near Horeb. The moving story of how God appeared to Moses from the flames of a burning bush and called him once again to lead the people of Israel out of Egypt is familiar. But hidden in the great truth of God's faithfulness is the lesson of Moses' faith in God that enabled him to stay the course for forty years in the wilderness while he waited for God.

Trusting God allowed me to relax in terms of what I was to do next in ministry. I felt little compulsion to follow my natural instinct to begin networking to find a new ministry and source of income. However, God gave me a strong sense of certainty that he would provide for us in another way. The next few weeks after my resignation, I was amazed at the number of unsolicited phone calls and letters I received from friends and acquaintances. All offered prayer, and many gave suggestions or proffered assistance with making contacts for a ministry position. God had reassured us that, like Moses, we were not forgotten.

I learned anew that God's responsibility is to meet our every need, while our responsibility is to trust him. That's not to say that the way God provides will be the same in every situation. Trusting God may have led someone else to begin making phone calls and writing letters. In our case it was just the opposite. I would have preferred to take some action, but God said, "Wait and trust, and watch what I will do."

No one is blameless

In marriage counseling I often find it necessary to play the role of judge or mediator in disputes between husband and wife. I point out to couples that they both bear responsibility for their problems. Often it's hard for a couple to hear that, but until they do there isn't much hope for getting the marriage back on track.

The same was true for me. In the months that followed my resignation, I began to recognize the role I had played in the debacle. It was easy to lay everything at the doorstep of my opposition—to blame the failures of the board or the silence of the staff or the lack of support from the congregation. But it didn't help me work through the pain. It wasn't until a friend made the offhanded comment "I guess by now you've figured out what you did wrong in all of this, too" that I began to look inward.

I thought about his casual remark for the rest of our lunch hour. I knew I had to think about what my role had been in the mess.

The Holy Spirit began to bring to mind several areas where I had failed; the few families who had engineered my departure weren't alone in their failures. I had a few of my own.

For example, God showed me that I had not done all I could to care for one of the antagonistic families when their son went through a serious accident. I hadn't handled a budget crisis well. I shouldn't have been so quick to express my opinions about issues that were largely inconsequential. My list of failures continued to grow as the Holy Spirit worked in my heart. None of the mistakes on the list were grave in themselves. But taken together, they began to tell a story I could not deny—I had contributed to the situation. I had to come to terms with those failures.

Acknowledgment and confession allowed me to experience God's forgiveness, which in turn set me free to begin the process of forgiving others.

Deeper compassion

Suffering has a way of helping us deepen our compassion for others who suffer. Jesus is the only person who ever lived who didn't need to grow in his ability to be compassionate to those in need. To him it came naturally and in full measure. That has not been so in my life.

I have become more sensitive to others who are hurting. When someone tells me of pain and hurt in her life, I often find my eyes filling with tears. Narrating a story of someone's brokenness in a sermon can also bring tears to my eyes.

While preaching a series on the life of David, I discovered this same process had occurred in David's life as a result of his broken relationship with his son Absalom. In *Leap Over a Wall*, Eugene Peterson writes, "The worst rejection of his life precipitated the most wonderful love—love for Absalom." Through the pain of estrangement from Absalom, David "recovered his extraordinary capacity to love."*

David's newfound compassion must have startled everyone. Who expected him to respond to Absalom's coup by mustering the troops and sending them into

*Eugene H. Peterson, *Leap Over a Wall* (New York: HarperCollins, 1998).

battle with the warning to his commanders that they were not to kill Absalom? David cautioned them, "Be gentle with the young man Absalom for my sake" (2 Sam. 18:5).

Was this an irrationally sentimental command? Or was it the result of God's extraordinary work in that man's heart, giving him a greater capacity for compassion? The Scripture leaves little doubt that the king's lament for his fallen son Absalom was an authentic expression of compassion, learned through the pain of his son's rebellion. Listen to David's lament: "O my son Absalom! My son, my son Absalom! If only I had died instead of you—O Absalom, my son, my son!" (2 Sam. 18:33).

Richard DeHaan tells the story of a man who was listening to others share their favorite Scripture passage with the congregation. Most of the verses spoke of salvation, assurance, or God's provision. Finally, an elderly man stood up to take his turn. He said that his favorite words in the Bible were "It came to pass." He explained, "When sickness strikes, it encourages me to know that it will pass. When I find myself in trouble, I know it won't last forever. I'll soon be able to say, 'It came to pass.'"

Although this man had inferred a different meaning from those words than the writers of Scripture intended, he saw in them an important truth that is found in the Bible: no matter how unending a trial may seem or how intense the pain we experience, the day will come when it will no longer be a burden or a source of distress. In fact, it will seem like nothing in the light of eternity. Second Corinthians 4:17 speaks of our "light and momentary troubles . . . achieving for us an eternal glory that far outweighs them all."

Years after the most intense pain of my ministry, I can now look back and say with the apostle Paul that I was "struck down, but not destroyed. We always carry around in our body the death of Jesus, so that the life of Jesus may also be revealed in our body" (2 Cor. 4:9–10).

A couple of years ago a particular family started attending our church. The wife told me, "We're here to recover from the battles my husband has had with fellow missionaries." I listened to the couple's stories of conflict with the co-workers they thought were their friends. The couple felt misunderstood and hurt. They needed a place to heal from their wounds.

I must admit their presence in the church caught me off guard. Not long after that conversation, an executive from their mission headquarters called me, asking, "Would your church be willing to work with us to develop a plan to help this family recover?"

The memory of how one church had cared for me and my family after my being forced out of a church several years earlier came rushing back. I am still in the pastorate because of the compassion of that church. Its pastor, although he knew of our situation, didn't publicly welcome us or rush us to get involved. He gave us anonymity. I needed that. I needed emotional space from the pounding our family had taken. He didn't even ask me to tell him what happened.

Within a short time after our family began attending the church, several small groups invited us to join. It was a gracious, low-key way for people in the church to let us know they cared. I explained to the small group leaders that Suzanne and I weren't ready for that level of intimacy. Two leaders said they would check back with me periodically. They offered to take the initiative. I appreciated that, for I didn't have much initiative left in me.

After several months I began to want to serve again. One Sunday I mentioned this to the pastor, and the next Wednesday the associate pastor called and asked if I wanted to substitute-teach for an adult Bible class on Sunday morning. I did.

Then, not long after that, a church elder, whom I had known before coming to the church, invited me to lunch. He surprised me by asking if I would consider joining the staff at the church as an associate pastor. Exactly thirty days after that lunch, I sat in a staff meeting as pastor of adult ministries. I had been frank with the senior pastor, saying, "I'm interested in the position, but I don't see myself as an associate pastor long-term."

"Whether it's six months or six years," the pastor said, "my goal is to see God bring you back into ministry."

I spent two years on staff at that church, and when I left, I prayed that God would give me the chance to do for someone what that church did for me.

When the hurting missionary family arrived at our church, I had my chance. That family joined our church and the husband ended up coming on staff for a year. When he left, he said, "Thank you for letting me experience what healthy relationships can be like."

The church, which has so much potential for inflicting pain on a pastor and his family, also has great potential for being an instrument of healing, for restoring vision for ministry. If nothing else, the suffering I've experienced at the hands of churches has forced me to think of others. The character forged from conflict, in the end, isn't about handling better my pain; it's about taking on the suffering of others.

Thank you for selecting a book from
BETHANY HOUSE PUBLISHERS

Bethany House Publishers is a ministry of Bethany Fellowship
International, an interdenominational, nonprofit organization
committed to spreading the Good News of Jesus Christ around
the world through evangelism, church planting, literature
distribution, and care for those in need. Missionary training is
offered through Bethany College of Missions.

Bethany Fellowship International is a member of the National
Association of Evangelicals and subscribes to its statement of
faith. If you would like further information, please contact:

Bethany Fellowship International
6820 Auto Club Road
Minneapolis, MN 55438 USA